OLYSLAGER AUTO LIBRARY

Cross-Country Cars
from 1945

compiled by the OLYSLAGER ORGANISATION

edited by Bart H. Vanderveen

FREDERICK WARNE & Co Ltd
London and New York

THE OLYSLAGER AUTO LIBRARY

This book is one of a growing range of titles on major transport subjects.
Titles published so far include:

The Jeep
Cross-Country Cars from 1945
Half-Tracks
Scammell Vehicles
Tanks and Transport Vehicles of World War II
Fire-Fighting Vehicles
Earthmoving Vehicles
Wreckers and Recovery Vehicles
Passenger Vehicles 1893–1940
Buses and Coaches from 1940
Fairground and Circus Transport

American Cars of the 1930s
American Cars of the 1940s
American Cars of the 1950s
American Trucks of the Early Thirties
American Trucks of the Late Thirties

British Cars of the Early Thirties
British Cars of the Late Thirties
British Cars of the Early Forties
British Cars of the Late Forties
British Cars of the Early Fifties
British Cars of the Late Fifties

Library of Congress Catalog Card No. 74-21048

ISBN 0 7232 1823 4

Filmset and printed in Great Britain by
BAS Printers Limited, Wallop, Hampshire

INTRODUCTION

The light cross-country vehicles as we have known them during the past three decades were initiated by the immensely successful US ¼-ton 4 × 4 military multi-purpose vehicle of the Second World War, which was and is popularly known as the 'Jeep'. This once ubiquitous vehicle was designed by Willys-Overland and mass-produced by them and, under a special agreement, the Ford Motor Co. (for full details about these, as well as other similar vehicles produced in the USA during the war, see *The Jeep* in this series and *The Observer's Fighting Vehicles Directory—World War II*). After the war, Willys-Overland registered the name Jeep as a trade mark and the exclusive use of it has been jealously guarded ever since by this company and its successors, viz. Willys Motors, Inc. from 1953, Kaiser Jeep Corp. from 1963 and Jeep Corp. (Subsidiary of American Motors Corp.) from 1970. It is therefore incorrect to use the name Jeep for any similar vehicles produced since 1945 by other than the above-mentioned companies and their various licencees. Although in the past several competitors have used the name Jeep in their sales literature, this has now long ceased and those manufacturers who offer similar vehicles have given them different names, examples being Land-Rover, Land Cruiser, Patrol, Campagnola, and many more. An alternative short generic name as good as 'Jeep' has, however, never been invented.

Originally, post-war vehicles in this lightweight, all-wheel drive, multi-purpose category, were aimed mainly at military and agricultural customers, but gradually they were bought in increasing numbers by private individuals for both daily transport and weekend leisure activities, as well as caravan, horsebox and boat towing and numerous other purposes. This civilian market has grown considerably, particularly in the United States where International, Ford, General Motors (Chevrolet, GMC) and Chrysler (Dodge, Plymouth), in that chronological order, introduced off-road vehicles to compete with the Jeep in the leisure market. In 1970 the US industry sold some 62,000 such vehicles and in 1972 this figure had nearly doubled, at 122,000. During 1973, 143,000 units were sold and the market is still expanding. Oddly enough, vehicles in this category are commonly known in the USA as '4WD', rather than 4 × 4, and often even as 'Four Wheelers'. The former designation could

equally apply to a 6 × 4, the latter to any 4 × 2! American manufacturers usually call them Sports Utility Vehicles, but, as explained earlier, there is no generally-accepted short name to cover all the different makes and models. With their various off-road vehicles several manufacturers offer vast ranges of factory-installed options such as alternative engines, transmissions, axles, tyres, etc., as well as bolt-on accessories, and a whole industry has sprung up to supply just about every additional gadget and piece of equipment the owners want or need to customize or improve their vehicles and/or to adapt them for rallying and short- and long-distance off-road racing. The latter sport is gaining considerably in popularity, not only in North America (California in particular) but also in Europe.

Meanwhile, although the public's attention was increasingly drawn to cross-country fun cars and recreational vehicles, the military authorities did not sit still. To replace their ageing Second World War vintage 'Jeeps' and immediate post-war successors the Americans developed the M151; the British had their 'Champ' but replaced it by the Land-Rover and France, Germany and Italy, after using several designs of their own, in 1966 started trilateral developments of a new common NATO ½-ton 4 × 4 amphibious vehicle. Many of these, however, tend to be so heavy, sophisticated and costly that a new bottom-end market was created for light economical and simple utility vehicles such as the VW 181, DAF 66YA, etc. Many armies buy and operate off-the-shelf civilian type 4 × 4 vehicles as well, if not exclusively.

This book provides the most comprehensive coverage ever published of post-1945 4 × 4 and 4 × 2 utility vehicles and cross-country cars, both civilian and military, and includes nearly 250 illustrations of models produced in more than 25 countries. The vehicles are arranged by make, in alphabetical order, and to facilitate cross-reference the index at the end of the book lists makes as well as model names. For additional coverage of military vehicles in these categories readers are referred to *The Observer's Military Vehicles Directory—from 1945*.

Piet Olyslager MSIA, MSAE, KIVI

ACKNOWLEDGEMENTS

This book was compiled and written largely from material in the libraries of the Olyslager Organisation and the editor. Additional photographs were kindly provided by several manufacturers as well as some private collectors, notably Jean-Gabriel Jeudy, Clifford Lake, Yasuo Ohtsuka and Laurie A. Wright.

ALFA ROMEO

4A Alfa Romeo 1900R

4A: **Alfa Romeo** of Milan, Italy, introduced the prototype for their first post-war field car in 1950. Dubbed *'la Folle'* it was a 6-seater, powered by a derated version of the contemporary Alfa Romeo 1900 car engine. Front suspension was independent. Although clearly patterned on the wartime American 'Jeep' the Alfa (and most other similar vehicles) featured bodywork of the type used by Rover in England for their Land-Rover (*q.v.*), i.e. a box-type body with rectangular side doors and a tail gate.

4B Alfa Romeo 1900M AR51/52

4C Alfa Romeo 1900M AR52

4B: **Alfa Romeo** 1900M *'Matta'* was the model that went into quantity production. From 1951 it was supplied to the Italian Army, designated AR51 (*Autovettura da Ricognizione*, 1951) and subsequently it was adopted by the Air Force (as AR52) and the Police. It was also available commercially. The 1884-cc (82·55 × 88 mm) twin-OHC 4-cyl. Model AR1307 engine had dry-sump lubrication and with 7:1 CR developed 65 (70 gross) bhp at 4400 rpm. Transmission was 4F1R with 2-speed transfer case. Front suspension was by wishbones and torsion bars; the live rear axle had semi-elliptic leaf springs. There was seating for two in the front and four, facing each other, in the rear. Tyre size was 6·00 or 6·40-16. This survivor, looking a little the worse for wear, was spotted on the slopes of Mount Etna, Sicily, in 1973. Note the rearward-opening door.

4C: **Alfa Romeo** 1900M AR52 of 1953/54, a civilian-operated model with hard-top. Station wagon and truck bodywork was also offered. Production ceased in 1955, after 2050 units had been delivered (2000 to the armed forces and the police, 50 to civilian customers). Originally the maximum speed quoted for the civilian edition was 120 km/h (*v.* 105 km/h for the military versions).

5B American Motors M422

5B: **American Motors** acquired exclusive manufacturing and sales rights for the 'Mighty Mite' in November 1954. Quantity production for the US Marine Corps commenced in April 1960 and until January 1963 nearly 4000 were delivered. They differed from the pilot models in many respects and were officially designated Truck, ¼-ton, 4 × 4, Utility, Lightweight, M422 and M422A1 (the latter was a somewhat modified version). On these models the front-wheel drive could be disengaged.

5A MARCO 'Mighty Mite'

5A: In 1950 American veteran racing driver Ben F. Gregory completed his design for a small 4 × 4 vehicle, dubbed the 'Mighty Mite'. Pilot models were built by the Mid-American Research Corp. at Wheatland, Pa, and powered by a German Porsche 44-bhp flat-4 air-cooled engine. The drive-line comprised a 3-speed transmission with Hi-Lo range, no-spin differential and positive four-wheel drive at all times. With a wheelbase of only 64 in the 1496-lb car could be run on any three wheels and in emergency a wheel could be changed without the use of a jack. 12 prototypes were extensively tested by the US Marine Corps during the early 1950s.

5C AMC AV-108-4 engine

5C: **American Motors** M422 'Mighty Mite' featured a new lightweight (200-lb) air-cooled V-4-cyl. engine (90°) of 107·8 CID. It had a gross output of 55 bhp at 3600 rpm and had originally been designed and developed by AMC and ALCOA during 1950–54 for possible use in light cars, generating sets, etc.

ARO

6A ARO 240

6C ARO/UMM M461

6B ARO 243

6A: **ARO** 240 is the basic model of a range of light 4 × 4 cross-country vehicles produced by MICM Uzina Mecanica Muscel at Cimpulung, Rumania. The range was introduced in 1970 and became available for export two years later. The power unit, designated MAS-ARO L25, is a 2495-cc (97 × 84·4 mm) OHV 4-cyl., developing 80 bhp (net) at 4200 rpm. It has a 5-bearing crankshaft and drives through an all-synchromesh 4-speed gearbox with 2-speed transfer case. Front suspension is independent with wishbones and coil springs; the live rear axle has conventional leaf springs. The two-door bodywork seats eight and has a hinged tail board. ARO 241 is a four-door version, also with soft-top.

6B: **ARO** 243, basically similar to the ARO 240 but fitted with a hard-top. Another variant, the ARO 244, has four-door station wagon bodywork. Top speed is quoted as 104–110 km/h, depending on model.

6C: **ARO** M461 (formerly UMM M461) is similar to the Soviet GAZ-69 (q.v.), licence-produced in Rumania in the same factory as the ARO 240 Series. It differs from the GAZ-69 mainly in having an oversquare 2495-cc (97 × 85 mm) 70-bhp engine (Model M207 OHV Four) with 4-speed gearbox and single-speed transfer case. It was introduced in 1964 and renamed ARO in the early 1970s. The vehicle seats eight and has live axles with leaf springs. Production ceased in 1974.

7A: **Austin** Moke of 1960. This was one of the pilot models for a field car based on the Austin ADO15 front-wheel drive small car which had been launched in 1959 as the Austin Se7en (later Mini) and, with minor differences, the Morris Mini-Minor. The first Mokes had a 950-cc engine with better low-speed torque than the standard car and could run on low-grade petrol (octane rating of around 70). They were tested by the British Army, who required a lightweight vehicle.

7A Austin Moke

7C Austin Mini-Moke

7C: **Austin** Mini-Moke six-wheelers soon appeared, as did several other conversions and modifications. Eventually complete body kits were put on the market by private firms, enabling people to assemble their own Moke-type car utilizing Mini (and later also BMC 1100) mechanical components.

7B: **Austin** Mini-Moke of 1962/63 had $72\frac{1}{2}$-in wheelbase compared with the original Moke's 80-in and the body was of a new design. After military interest decreased BMC decided to make the Mini-Moke available to the public. Both Austin and Morris versions were introduced in August 1964, at a basic price of £335 (£407 incl. PT in the UK). These had the standard 848-cc 4-cyl. 'east-west' engine, albeit slightly detuned.

7D: In 1969 production of the Mini-Moke was transferred to British Leyland in Australia. With several modifications, incl. 13-in (v. 10-in) wheels, 1098-cc engine (1275-cc for export to USA), etc., it was marketed as the Moke from 1970. In 1972 the Australian Army ordered over 500, one of which is shown (official nomenclature: Truck, $\frac{1}{4}$-ton, CL, 4 × 2, Lightweight).

7B Austin Mini-Moke

7D British Leyland Moke (Australia)

AUSTIN/BLMC

8A: **Austin** 'Twini-Moke' was a twin-engined variant of the Mini-Moke. The first was produced in 1962 and consisted simply of a standard model in which the rear suspension/sub-frame was substituted by another complete front assembly. This 8-cyl. 1696-cc vehicle had tremendous performance but the two gearboxes had to be operated individually and cargo space was negligible. Some more were made in 1963 and in 1964; one with two 1098-cc engines was evaluated by the US Army Tank-Automotive Centre in Warren, Mich. The project was not pursued, however.

8B: **Austin** Ant appeared in 1966, first as an experimental air-transportable vehicle for the British Army. The power unit was derived from that of the contemporary Austin-Morris 1100 ADO16 car, with a 2-speed reduction gear incorporated in the gearbox. A third gear lever was provided to engage rear-wheel drive.

8C: **Austin** Ant pickup truck was a proposed commercial version of the air-transportable car. It was introduced in 1967 and a small number were made. Like the earlier model it had torsion bar suspension, independent front and rear. After the British Leyland amalgamation the Austin Ant project was transferred to Rover, but since the retail price would have been close to that of the Land-Rover the Ant's further development was discontinued.

8B Austin Ant

8A Austin 'Twini-Moke'

8C Austin Ant

9A Austin Champ

9A: **Austin** Champ, Model WN1, was the first standard post-war British Army ¼-ton 4 × 4 Combat Truck and was officially designated FV1801(A). The power unit was a standardized Rolls-Royce B-Series engine (B40, 4-cyl., 80-bhp, 2838-cc), driving through a 5-speed all-synchromesh gearbox. Forward/reverse gear change unit was incorporated in the rear differential, from where the front wheels were also driven. The front wheel drive declutch was in the front differential/final drive unit. The vehicle had independent torsion-bar front and rear suspension and was originally designed by the Nuffield Organization (*q.v.*). Austin obtained the production contract (prior to its subsequent merger with Nuffield), and built about 13,750, from November 1952 until 1955, in the Cofton Hackett Aero Factory, which was taken over by Austin from the Government for truck production (Champ ¼-ton, K9WD 1-ton 4 × 4, etc.). The Champ was also available with Austin's own 2·2-litre A90 engine, for military and civilian purposes but few of these were produced.

9B/C: **Austin** Champ with RR engine was waterproofed and could safely be taken into depths up to 6 ft.

9D: **Austin** Champ FV1802(A) variant of 1954 had doors, hinged tailboard and lengthwise rear seats. This rare model, which was never produced in quantity, is now civilian-owned. Many standard-type Champs are also in the hands of civilian enthusiasts, both at home and abroad.

9B/C Austin Champ

9D Austin Champ

10A Austin Champ

10C Austin Gipsy Series I

10B Austin Champ

10A: **Austin** Champ was in British Army service from 1952 to the mid-1960s, when thousands were released to Civvy Street via the Government auction sales at Ruddington near Nottingham. Shown is a typical civilian application in the form of a light recovery/service vehicle, fitted with an Austin truck cab. It was operated by an Okehampton, Devon, garage.

10B: **Austin** Champ as a 'road locomotive', used in the Dutch Veluwe area, 1970. Many 'de-mobbed' Champs, originating from the British Army in Germany, remained on the Continent. Others were exported, e.g. to Australia.

10C: **Austin** Gipsy was Austin's answer to Rover's Land-Rover and was first made in 1957. The Series I (shown) was available with petrol and diesel engine, both 2·2-litre 4-cyl. units, of 62 and 55 bhp respectively. It replaced the Champ in its civilian guise and featured trailing arm-type independent front and rear suspension mounted on Flexitor rubber units. The latter comprised a tube upon which the arm was mounted, moulded into a rubber torsional assembly. Wheelbase was 90 in. Series I production ceased in the autumn of 1959.

11A Austin Gipsy Series II

11B Austin Gipsy Series IV GM4M10

11A: Austin Gipsy Series II appeared in January 1960 and had various detail modifications. The Flexitor rubber suspension was improved and two- and four-wheel drive could now be used with transfer case high and low ratio (low only on Series I). Petrol and diesel versions were again available, as were numerous optional extras. In addition to the standard model shown, there was now a long-wheelbase (111-in) version, which had a conventional rear axle with leaf springs. Series II models were in production until August 1962.

11B: Austin Gipsy Series IV (there was no Series III) range was introduced in September 1962. SWB (90-in) models were designated GM4M10, LWB (111-in) models GM4M15. The most important distinguishing features of the Series IV were a restyled driving compartment and radiator grille, and the availability of leaf-sprung live axles, front and rear, on all models. In June 1965 the unsuccessful Flexitor rubber suspension system was dropped for good.

11C: Austin Gipsy Series IV Model GM4M15 long-wheelbase export model with hard-top and rear side windows. Picture was taken in Switzerland in 1966. In spite of the fact that the Gipsy was now very much like the Land-Rover, it still sold badly. Moreover, in 1967 Rover became a subsidiary of Leyland which in 1968 amalgamated with British Motor Holdings to form the British Leyland Motor Corporation. Austin also being part of this combine it seemed pointless to continue the Gipsy and the range was phased out during mid-1968.

11C Austin Gipsy Series IV GM4M15

AUTOCARS, AUTO UNION

12A Autocars Dragoon

12C Auto Union Munga

12A: Autocars Company Ltd. of Tirat Carmel, near Haifa in Israel, in 1967 commenced production of a light cross-country vehicle named Dragoon. Designed by Standard-Triumph in England, it utilized the engine/transmission unit of the Triumph 1300/1500 front-wheel drive car (*see* Triumph Pony). Normal front-wheel drive on the Dragoon, which has a De Dion-type leaf-sprung front axle, provides four speeds in high auxiliary range; selection of four-wheel drive (i.e. engagement of the rear axle drive) also engages low ratio, giving four speeds in low range. Rear axle is of the conventional leaf-sprung live type. Made mainly as a pickup truck, the Dragoon was offered also with four-door superstructure and full-length canvas top. It was exported to Greece and Switzerland and assembly took place in Persia.

12B Auto Union Munga

12B: Auto Union Munga was introduced in 1955 as one of three prototypes for a cross-country car for the new German *Bundeswehr* (the other two were submitted by Goliath and Porsche). After testing and modifications it went into quantity production in December 1956. Shown is one of the pilot models, which had a 38-bhp 3-cyl. 2-stroke engine of 897 cc. The name Munga was an abbreviation of *Mehrzweck Universal Geländewagen mit Allradantrieb* (multi-purpose universal field car with all-wheel drive) and was introduced somewhat later when the car became commercially available.

12C: Auto Union Munga chassis had a narrow ladder-type frame with independent suspension, identical front and rear. Production models had a 40-bhp engine (44-bhp 980-cc from late 1958). Except for very early models all had permanent positive four-wheel drive. Auto Union occasionally used their old-established marque name DKW for the Munga, especially during the first years of its production.

13A Auto Union Munga 6

13A/B: **Auto Union** Munga F91/6 3036 6-seater appeared in August 1958 and was basically similar to the contemporary F91/4 3035 4-seater. Instead of the latter's '*Kübel*'-type body it had seating for four persons in the rear compartment. It was produced, with the 40-bhp 897-cc 3-cyl. 2-stroke engine, until early 1959. Wheelbase and overall length were the same, at 2·00 and 3·45 m. The Munga also appeared with a hard-top body and with a truck cab. Optional extras included power take-off, 1·5-ton winch, etc.

13C: **Auto Union** Munga 4-seater in its final form : Model F91/4/1000 3038 with 980-cc engine. As such it was in production from November 1958 until December 1968. It was also known as the Munga 4. Large numbers of these were used by the German Army as well as the armed forces of some other countries (incl. the British Army in Berlin and the Netherlands Army and Air Force).

13D: **Auto Union** Munga 8 8-seater (shown) and Munga 6 6-seater were made with the 44-bhp (50 gross) 980-cc engine from February 1962 until December 1968. Both were supplied for military and civilian use and had lengthwise rear seats, a tail gate and side-mounted spare wheel.

13B Auto Union Munga 6

13C Auto Union Munga 4

13D Auto Union Munga 8

BMW, BORGWARD

14A BMW/Glas

14A: **BMW** in 1967 took over Hans Glas GmbH of Dingolfing, Germany, who at that time were experimenting with a prototype for a new ½-ton 4 × 4 amphibious cross-country vehicle, powered by a BMW 2000 engine. In 1971 BMW produced an improved edition, but this also remained in the experimental stage. They were but a few of numerous prototypes for a new NATO general purpose vehicle. Illustrated is the 1967/68 Glas/BMW, climbing ashore after an amphibious test.

14B: **Borgward** was one of the major suppliers of cross-country vehicles for the German *Bundeswehr* from 1955 until 1961. Most of these vehicles were 9-seater personnel carriers and ¾-ton trucks, based on a standard 3·20-m wheelbase chassis with 80-bhp 6-cyl. engine of 2337 cc with 4F1R × 2 transmission, live axles and 9·00-16 tyres. In addition there was a 3·40-m wheelbase chassis with 10·00-20 tyres for 1½-ton trucks. Examples of all three types are shown (right to left).

14C: **Borgward** 9-seater, three-quarter rear view, showing the large rear locker. This locker provided considerably more load space than in comparable vehicles built for the *Wehrmacht* in the Second World War (Mercedes-Benz, Steyr, etc.). The Borgward model designation for this vehicle was B2000A/O; in the German Army it was known as *Lkw 0,75 t gl* or *Neunsitzer* (9-seater). When Büssing took over the Borgward factory in 1961/62 they continued its production until 1968; during this period a further 168 units were delivered. Many were used for driving instruction purposes. They were in service also with the *Bundesgrenzschutz*; some of these had a hard-top on the rear passenger compartment.

14B Borgward B2000A/O and B2500A/O

14C Borgward/Büssing B2000A/O

15A Chevrolet Blazer

15B Chevrolet Blazer

15A : **Chevrolet** introduced their Blazer off-road Sports Utility car in April 1969 as their answer to the Jeep, the Ford Bronco and the International Scout. As *Motor Trend* put it at the time : 'Ol' Number One is now involved, so there must be something to this four-wheel-drive, off-the-road epidemic'. The Blazer was designed as a simple basic (by US standards) open unit with a single seat for the driver. From that base, the buyer could tailor the Blazer to his particular desires from a wide range of options and body colours. It was strongly constructed with a heavy channel steel frame, leaf-sprung live axles, 104-in wheelbase and rigid single-unit body. Among the long list of options were a soft-top, a removable fibreglass hard-top, front passenger seat, full-width rear seat, three engines, three transmissions, power steering and brakes, air conditioning, etc. For severe usage, heavy-duty springs, shock absorbers, clutch, radiator and tyres were available. Provision for PTO was standard.

15B : **Chevrolet** Blazer 1972 in hard-top/station wagon form. It was offered in 6- and V-8-cyl. models of 250 and 307 CID respectively. A 350 CID V8 was optional. In addition to the standard 3-speed manual transmission there were a 4-speed manual and 3-speed automatic. Transfer case was 2-speed. From 1970 4 × 2 versions were available. Chevrolet also offered Suburban Carryall and other body styles on 4 × 4 light truck chassis.

15C : **Chevrolet** Blazer for 1973 was restyled and had 106·5-in wheelbase and other modifications. Engine options were 250 CID Six and 350 CID V8, the latter in conjunction with full-time all-wheel drive with lockable centre differential. The 1974 model, which was similar, is shown, with the optional hard-top.

15C Chevrolet Blazer

CITROËN

16A Citroën 2CV 4 × 4 Sahara

16A: **Citroën** 2CV 4 × 4 was a twin-engined version of the famous *Deux Chevaux* car and was known as the Sahara. Based on the 425-cc twin-cylinder standard car, a second power unit was mounted in the rear, driving the rear wheels; if not required the rear-wheel drive could be 'disengaged' by the flick of a lever adjacent to the conventionally located common gear lever and switching off the rear engine. Except for the accelerator, clutch and gearbox controls the two engines were entirely separate, each having its own ignition switch, dynamo charging light, fuel tank, etc. Citroën first built the 2CV 4 × 4 in 1959, but similar conversions have been carried out by private individuals (albeit usually by welding two front halves together!).

16C: **Citroën** Mehari appeared in June, 1968, and is based on the company's Dyane 6 car chassis. It has a Cycolac ABS thermoplastic body and the shell is assembled from 11 bolt-on panels. The vehicle is powered by a 602-cc 28-bhp air-cooled flat-twin engine, driving the front wheels through a 4-speed all-synchromesh gearbox. Vehicle weighs about 585 kg and measures 3·58 × 1·53 × 1·59 m. Wheelbase is 2·40 m, tyre size 135 × 380. Picture was taken during the *'Raid 1971'* Citroën rally. Commercially available it is also used by the French Army, Air Force, Navy and Gendarmerie.

16B Citroën 2CV 4 × 4 Sahara

16B: **Citroën** 2CV 4 × 4 Sahara was equally useful in snow as in soft sand and muddy terrain. Picture shows a snow-plough attachment.

16C Citroën Mehari

COURNIL, CREUSOT-LOIRE

17A: Cournil (or: Tracteur Cournil) cross-country cars were produced by Ets. Bernard Cournil of Aurillac, Cantal, France. About a thousand were built, during 1960–70. Various types of power units were used, including Hotchkiss and Renault petrol engines and Hotchkiss and Indenor diesels. Model shown had a 2·26-litre 4-cyl. Hotchkiss diesel engine of 35 bhp at 1800 rpm. Transmission was 3F1R with 2-speed transfer box. Some had a winch. The vehicle weighed 870 kg, had 7·00-16 tyres and an overall length and width of 3·45 × 1·58 m. There was also a long-wheelbase 6-seater. Some were used by fire brigades in the South-east of France (Marseilles, etc.)

17B: Creusot-Loire Bison was a versatile French military amphibious multi-purpose vehicle. In 1967 the marque name was SFAC (Société des Forges et Ateliers du Creusot—Usines Schneider). It could be used as a personnel carrier, seating six men plus driver, or as a weapons carrier, launching platform for anti-tank missiles, ambulance, tractor, supply carrier, etc. The power unit was a 4152-cc 100-bhp air-cooled Saviem Chabay flat-4, derated to 85/90 bhp.

17C: One of the prototypes of the Bison VB100 4 × 4 *Véhicule de servitude* was built by the firm of Batignolles-Chatillon, about 1964. It was designed by M. Bouffort, under whose licence the vehicles were produced.

17B Creusot-Loire Bison

17A Cournil

17C Bison VB100

DAF

18A DAF YA054

18B DAF YA054

18A/B: **DAF** YA054 was an experimental cross-country 4-seater, produced in 1951/52. It was intended to replace the US 'Jeep' in the Netherlands Army but remained in the prototype stage. From a central differential the wheels were driven by propeller shafts which ran fore and aft outside the chassis frame. Suspension was by trailing arms with torsion bars at front, coil springs at rear. The engine was an American 3·1-litre 4-cyl. Hercules JX4C petrol unit of 60 bhp at 3200 rpm. The transmission comprised a 3F1R main gearbox with 2-speed auxiliary unit (0·93 and 2·36 to 1). The wheelbase was 2·20 m.

18C: **DAF** 66YA (originally known as 55YA), developed in 1972 from the contemporary DAF 66 car with Renault/DAF 1108-cc 4-cyl. engine, is a military 0·4-ton 4 × 2 car, intended to replace or supplement $\frac{1}{4}$-ton 4 × 4 vehicles in those roles where four-wheel drive is not required. Like the DAF 66 car it features Variomatic automatic transmission with a differential and De Dion-type rear axle. A differential lock is available, which improves the vehicle's modest cross-country performance. Maximum road speed is 115 km/h, weight about 870 kg, wheelbase 2·25 m. At the front the car has independent suspension and disc brakes. The Netherlands Army placed an order for 1200 units in late 1972.

18C DAF 66YA

19A Daihatsu Taft .

19A: **Daihatsu** Taft 4 × 4 F10 4- and FT10L 6-seater (shown) from Japan have an integral roll-over bar, 2·02-m wb, 6·00-16 tyres, 58-bhp 958-cc 4-cyl. engine, and 4F1R × 2 transmission. Introduced in 1974.

19B Delahaye VLR

19D Delahaye VLR(D)

19C Delahaye VLR(D)

19B: **Delahaye** introduced a 4 × 4 military utility vehicle in 1949/50. Peugeot (*q.v.*) introduced a similar but simpler vehicle but the Delahaye was accepted for series production, albeit in modified form. It featured independent front and rear suspension, with trailing arms and torsion bars, identical in configuration to that of the German Volkswagen.

19C/D: **Delahaye** VLR (*Voiture de Liaison et de Reconnaissance*), production models of 1951/52 were also known as the VLRD (VLR Delahaye), or officially, 'VLR 4 × 4 Delahaye 0,4 t Mle 51'. On early models the headlamps were behind the radiator grille. Compared with the 1949/50 prototype (19B) the bodywork was completely redesigned. The engine was a 4-cyl. OHV Delahaye petrol unit of 1992 cc with dry-sump lubrication system and developing 58 bhp (63 gross). The transmission comprised a 4-speed main and 2-speed auxiliary gearbox. Diff locks were provided. Wheelbase was 2·15 m, overall length 3·46 m, weight approx. 1400 kg. Fig. 19C shows one of six units which were entered by the French Army in the 1951 Mediterranean-Cape Town Rally.

DELAHAYE

20A Delahaye VLR(D)

20B Delahaye VLR(D)

20C Delahaye 171

20A: **Delahaye** VLR *Tous Terrains* was available commercially from 1951 but the bulk of its production was for the French Army (where it was later superseded by the licence-built Second World War type Willys Jeep; *see* Hotchkiss).

20B: **Delahaye** VLRs were largely disposed of by the French Army during the 1960s and many ended up with farmers and other civilian customers. This specimen, nicely restored and kept, was photographed in France in 1971. Very few found their way abroad.

20C: **Delahaye** Model 171 was a 1-ton heavy-duty chassis, available with pickup truck, ambulance and *Break* (shown) bodywork. It was produced during 1949–53 and had a 6-cyl. OHV engine of 3557 cc, developing 100 bhp at 3500 rpm. Drive was to the rear axle only, through a 4-speed gearbox, but the specialist firm of Herwaythorn offered a four-wheel drive conversion. The 4 × 2 *Break* measured 5·22 × 1·93 × 2·30 m; wheelbase was 3·20 m, tyre size 9·00-16.

DODGE, FARMOBIL, FART

21A Dodge Power Wagon

21B Dodge Ramcharger

21A: **Dodge** Power Wagon 108-in wb 4 × 4 light truck chassis of 1959 with Town Wagon personnel-carrying body. Engine options 120-bhp Six or 205-bhp V8. GVW 6000 lb. This is just one example of the countless Power Wagon vehicles produced by the Chrysler Corporation. They were sold also under the De Soto and Fargo trade names.

21B: **Dodge** introduced their Ramcharger 4 × 4 Sports Utility vehicle in February 1974. Similar in general configuration to the Chevrolet Blazer, Ford Bronco, International Scout, etc., it is also available as Plymouth Trail Duster (q.v.). Both have 106-in wb and measure 184·6 by 79·5 in. Standard engine is a 155-bhp 318 CID V8 ; optional are higher-powered V8s of 360, 400 and 440 CID. Transmission options include 3F1R manual (standard), 4F1R manual and 3F1R automatic. There are two optional roofs, white vinyl and steel hard-top. Many other options are available. Four-wheel drive is permanent, through a lockable centre differential in the 2-speed transfer case.

21C Farmobil

21D FART Breack

21C: **Farmobil** was a multi-purpose vehicle shaped like the Steyr-Puch Haflinger (q.v.) but of simpler design and without front-wheel drive. The rear wheels were driven by an air-cooled flat-twin 35-bhp BMW 700 engine, mounted at the rear. Designed and developed in 1959/60 by Fahr of West Germany the Farmobil was produced by Farco, a Greek company which in 1963 was taken over by Chrysler. In Germany it was reintroduced in 1965 as BMW Farmobil, BMW having acquired sole marketing rights in the Federal Republic.

21D: **FART** Breack (or Break) 4 × 2 4-seater was launched by Fabrica Autoveicoli Rimorchi Torino, Italy, in 1965. It was based on Fiat 500 Giardiniera mechanical components with extra gear reduction and dual tyres front and rear. Its top speed was about 65 km/h, gradeability about 40%.

FERVES, FIAT

22A/B Ferves Ranger

22C: **Fiat** introduced a military type field car in 1950, concurrently with Alfa Romeo (*q.v.*). It was powered by a long-stroke 1901-cc version of the contemporary Fiat 1400 car engine, driving through a 4F1R gearbox with 2-speed transfer case.

22C Fiat 1900

22D: **Fiat** Campagnola was the name given to the civilian version of the 6-seater production model, made from 1951. The first military version went into quantity production as *Autovettura de Ricognizione Fiat AR51*. Compared with the prototype (22C) they featured many detail changes. Note how the doors are rear-hinged and fixed in the fully-open position. Tyre size was 6·40-16. From 1953 the civilian version was available with a 43-bhp 1901-cc Fiat diesel engine. A station wagon variant was also made.

22A/B: **Ferves** Ranger was a 4-seater field car, introduced in 1967 by Ferves s.r. of Turin, Italy. It had a Fiat 500 air-cooled twin-cylinder engine of 22 bhp (gross) with 4F1R gearbox, driving all four wheels. Suspension was independent, with coil springs front and rear. In addition to the Ranger there was the Cargo, which had a truck-type rear body. Both had 1·55-m wb and measured 2·83 × 1·45 m. By 1970 a 5F1R transmission was fitted, providing an extra-low ratio. A diff lock was available, as were 4 × 2 variants with 4- or 5-speed gearbox.

22D Fiat Campagnola

23A Fiat AR55, AR59

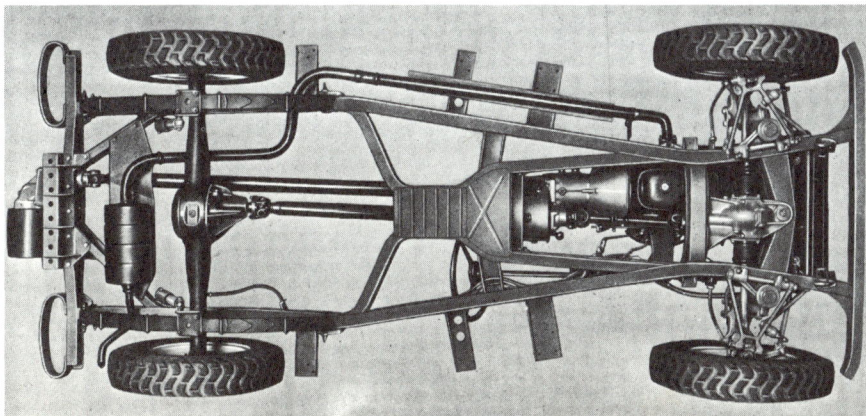

23C Fiat Campagnola (X-11/1)

23A : **Fiat** AR55 superseded the AR51 model in production in 1955. It was improved in various respects. The engine's maximum power output was increased from 53 to 59 bhp, road speed from 100 to about 115 km/h. In 1959 it became the AR59, with higher GVW rating and 24-Volt electrical system. The AR59 was in the NATO 0·5-ton class and was produced until the early 1970s.

23B : **Fiat** Campagnola 1951/52 chassis, viewed from underneath. Note the sturdy frame construction, the independent front suspension (with enclosed coil springs) and the optional PTO-driven belt pulley at the rear.

23C : **Fiat** introduced a prototype for a new cross-country car in 1973, designated X-11/1. In 1974 this became the new Campagnola. It features unitary body-cum-chassis construction with independent suspension front and rear and an 80-bhp (net) 2-litre petrol engine.

23D : **Fiat** co-operated with MAN of Germany and Saviem of France to design and develop a new 0·5-ton amphibious cross-country vehicle for use by various NATO countries. Another international consortium (Hotchkiss/Büssing/Lancia) worked on an alternative design. Work on these projects commenced in 1966. Shown is one of the Fiat/MAN/Saviem pilot models (1973).

23B Fiat Campagnola

23D FMS

FLETCHER, FMC

24A Fletcher

24B Fletcher Flair 115

24A: **Fletcher** Aviation Corp. of Pasadena, California, in 1953 launched a 6-seater semi-amphibious 4 × 4 vehicle, powered by a 1·5-litre 55-bhp Porsche air-cooled flat-4 engine. The suspension units were attached directly to the lightweight frameless hull. The engine was built by Fletcher under Porsche licence.

24B: **Fletcher** Flair 115 of 1954 was a development of the vehicle shown in Fig. 24A, again powered by a rear-mounted Porsche engine. It is shown here alongside the then standard US Army $\frac{1}{4}$-ton 4 × 4 Willys Jeep M38A1. The Fletcher vehicles did not reach the quantity production stage.

24C FMC XR311

24C: **FMC** Corporation's Ordnance Division of San Jose, California developed a 'dune buggy' type high-mobility vehicle, designated XR311, in 1971/72. Ten were purchased by the US Army's Land Warfare Laboratory for tests. Powered by a rear-mounted Chrysler V8 318 CID engine of 187 bhp at 4000 rpm, driving through a Chrysler 3-speed automatic transmission, the 3-seater 4800-lb basic vehicle can be adapted for various roles, incl. reconnaissance, command, convoy escort, military police, anti-armour, etc. The wheelbase is 121 in and the overall dimensions of the basic vehicle are 171 × 76 × 63 in. Acceleration time from 0–60 mph is 12 seconds, maximum speed 80 mph (on the level).

25A FN AS24

25A–D: **FN** *Véhicule Aeroporte* was produced by the Fabrique Nationale d'Armes de Guerre (later renamed Fabrique Nationale Herstal) of Herstal, near Liège in Belgium, under Straussler licence. Some 500 units were made in the early 1960s after the first pilot model had appeared in 1959. Prototypes had also been made in Britain and W. Germany. The AS24 is a very simple 3-wheeled vehicle, which can be 'folded' for air-drops by parachute. On reaching the ground it can be made operational in about one minute. It can carry either four armed men, sitting abreast, or driver plus 250 kg. An FN 2-cyl. 2-stroke engine of 243·5 cc drives the two rear wheels through a 4-speed gearbox, chain and differential. Tyres are 22 × 12 in Lypsoid type, with a pressure of only 6 to 7 lb/sq. in. Top speed with full load is 50 km/h. It is used by the Belgian and French armed forces.

25C FN AS24

25B FN AS24

25D FN AS24

FORD

26A Ford XM151

26B Ford XM151

26A: **Ford** Motor Company of the USA, after having co-produced the Willys 'Jeep' during 1942—45, was awarded a US Army contract in 1951 for the design and development of a new military $\frac{1}{4}$-ton 4 × 4 utility truck. Two design configurations were developed, one with a separate chassis frame and conventional live axles and one with unitary body construction and coil-spring independent suspension. The latter (XM151-2) was selected for further development. One of the first pilot models, dubbed 'Mutt' (Military Utility Tactical Truck) is shown. Quantity production of the final design (M151, see US Ordnance) commenced in 1960, contracts being awarded to Ford and, later, Kaiser Jeep and AM General Corp.

26B: **Ford** XM151 'Mutt' (a nickname which was later dropped) pilot model under test at US Army's Aberdeen Proving Ground, Maryland, in 1955. It had a new 141·5 CID 65-bhp (net) 4-cyl. engine with 4-speed transmission and single-speed transfer box (4F1R × 1). Wheelbase and overall length were 85 and 132 in respectively.

26C Ford Bronco

26C: **Ford** Bronco Sports Utility was first introduced in 1965 and was a civilian vehicle (unlike the M151, which was produced only for military use). Primarily a personal transportation and recreational vehicle, the Bronco proved a popular choice for the outdoor-minded. Illustrated is the basic model of 1965/66. It had a 105-bhp (gross) 170 CID 6-cyl. engine with 3F1R × 2 transmission. Axle ratio was 4·11 to 1 with 4·57 optional. Wheelbase was 92 in, overall length 152·1 in, width 68·8 in. Truck cab and full-length hard-top were available. Ford Motor Co. were the second US manufacturers (after International Harvester, q.v.) to start competing with Jeep in the 'leisure vehicle' market.

27A Ford Bronco

27B Ford Bronco

27B : **Ford** Bronco was available with optional automatic transmission for the first time for the 1973 model year. Basically the vehicle remained unchanged, however.

27C : **Ford** Broncos are extensively used in off-road races and similar competitions, particularly in North America. In most instances vehicles used for such events are extensively modified for maximum performance and safety. Broncos have done extremely well in traditional events such as the brutal Baja 500 and 1000 (on Mexico's Baja peninsula, just south of California). For the 1972 model year Ford offered the Baja Bronco (shown), a limited production version of the famous off-road racers driven by Parnelli Jones and Bill Stroppe.

27A : **Ford** Bronco for 1970/71 was still much the same as when it first appeared in 1965, but an alternative power unit was available in the form of a 302 CID V8 of 205 bhp (gross). The chassis was of conventional design with a box-section frame and wide-track (57·4 in) live axles. The front axle had Mono-Beam coil-spring suspension with forged-steel radius rods and track bar, the rear suspension was conventional, with leaf springs. At extra cost the rear axle, or both axles, could be fitted with a limited-slip differential. Tyre size was 7·35-15 or 6·50-16, GVW up to 4700 lb (Six) or 3900 lb (V8). Shown is the Sport Bronco Wagon with front-mounted electric winch, one of many optional extras.

27C Ford Baja Bronco

FREIGHTERS, FUJI, GAZ

28A Freighters Ami

28B Fuji/Subaru 1400 4WD

28A: **Freighters** Ami was developed in Australia in 1956 by Freighters Ltd, a company specializing in truck and bus bodies, trailers, etc. 5000 units were planned to be produced in their Melbourne plant, starting in early 1957 and to be marketed by Associated Motor Industries (AMI) of Sydney, but the project did not materialize. The car had a British 68-bhp Standard Vanguard engine with 3F1R × 2 transmission, torsion bar independent suspension and tubular steel frame.

28B: **Fuji** Heavy Industries Ltd of Japan launched their **Subaru** 1400 4WD station wagon (known in Japan as Leone) in 1974. It has a 4-cyl. 1361-cc 77-bhp engine with 4F1R gearbox, normally driving the front wheels. Rear-wheel drive may be engaged for extra traction when required. Wheelbase is 2·44 m, length 4·04 m.

28C GAZ-67(B)

28C: **GAZ**-67 was a Soviet-built 4 × 4 field car, introduced in 1942/43 and clearly patterned on the US 'Jeep' which was supplied to the Red Army in large quantities during the Second World War. After minor improvements it went into series production as GAZ-67B. It was made until 1953 and was of conventional design except for the front suspension which featured dual quarter-elliptic leaf springs, located above and below the live front axle.

28D: **GAZ**-67B and its armoured car derivative, the BA64 (or 'Bobby') had a GAZ-M1 4-cyl. 3·2-litre L-head engine of 54 bhp which was fundamentally the same as that of the US Ford Model A and B. This specimen, preserved in England, has an electric fuel pump and a few other modifications. The car measures 3·35 × 1·69 m and has a wheelbase of 2·10 m. Weight is 1320 kg, payload 400 kg.

28D GAZ-67B

29A : **GAZ**-M72 was a four-wheel drive variant of the conventional Pobieda (GAZ-M20) 4–5-seater car. It was produced by the Molotov Works at Gorky in the Soviet Union during 1955–58. The engine was a 52-bhp 4-cyl. L-head of 82 × 100 mm (2112 cc), driving through a 3-speed gearbox with 2-speed transfer case. Maximum road speed was 90 km/h, fuel consumption 14 litres per 100 km. Axle ground clearance 210 mm, track (tread) front 1·35 m, rear 1·39 m.

29A GAZ-M72

29B GAZ-69A(M)

29C GAZ-69(M)

29B : **GAZ**-69A 4-door 5-seater 4 × 4 field car first appeared in 1952 and remained in production for over two decades, with only minor changes. It had a 4-cyl. OHV engine of 2112 cc (82 × 100 mm) until 1967 when the bore was increased to 88 mm, increasing the cubic capacity to 2433 cc. Power output went up from 55 bhp at 3600 rpm to 65 at 3800. These later models were known as GAZ-69AM. In 1956 production had been transferred from Gorky to Ulyanovsk, where during the 1960s a replacement vehicle was developed (see UAZ-469). The GAZ-69(M) was of conventional design, with separate frame and leaf-sprung live axles. Transmission was 3F1R × 2. Post-1956 models —produced in Ulyanovsk—were also known as UAZ-69AM.

29C : **GAZ**-69 was a 2-door 6-seater variant of the GAZ-69A. It had a tail gate, lengthwise seats in the rear compartment and the spare wheel was mounted on the left-hand side, between driver's door and rear mudguard. It was produced simultaneously with the GAZ-69A and in 1967 was redesignated GAZ-69M. Radio-equipped specimen shown was used by the East German Army. It was licence-produced in Rumania as M461 (see ARO).

GEORGES IRAT, GMC

30A Georges Irat VDB

30A: Georges Irat, a famous French car builder during the period 1921–46, introduced the *Voiture du Bled* (field car) in 1951. Designed during the war by Ing. Emile Petit, it was produced by the Société Chérifienne d'Études des Automobiles Georges Irat of Bld Ballande, Casablanca (Morocco), until 1953. The little car was powered by a rear-mounted 28-bhp Panhard Dyna air-cooled 745-cc flat-twin engine, driving the rear wheels through a standard 3F1R Panhard gearbox plus a reduction gearbox, doubling the number of speeds. All wheels were suspended independently and the steering wheel was placed centrally. Wheelbase was 1·95 m, length and width 3·24 × 1·35 m.

30B: GMC Jimmy was first launched in October 1969, for the 1970 model year, Except for radiator grille and trim details, it was identical to the Chevrolet Blazer (*q.v.*), with 104-in wheelbase, leaf-sprung live axles, and 2-speed transfer case. Engines and transmissions were also the same: 250 CID Six as standard with 307 and 350 CID V8 options, 3-speed manual transmission standard, 4-speed manual and 3-speed automatic (Turbo Hydra-Matic) optional. Engine power output figures (gross/net) were 155/125, 200/157 and 255/200 bhp respectively.

30C: GMC Jimmy of 1970 fitted with optional removable fibreglass top. GMC also offered 4 × 4 light truck chassis with Suburban (station wagon) and pickup bodywork

30C GMC Jimmy

30B GMC Jimmy

30D: GMC Jimmy was restyled for 1973, along the same lines as the Chevrolet Blazer (*see* 15C). Shown is the 1974 edition, which was virtually unchanged. Full-time and conventional four-wheel drive are available.

30D GMC Jimmy

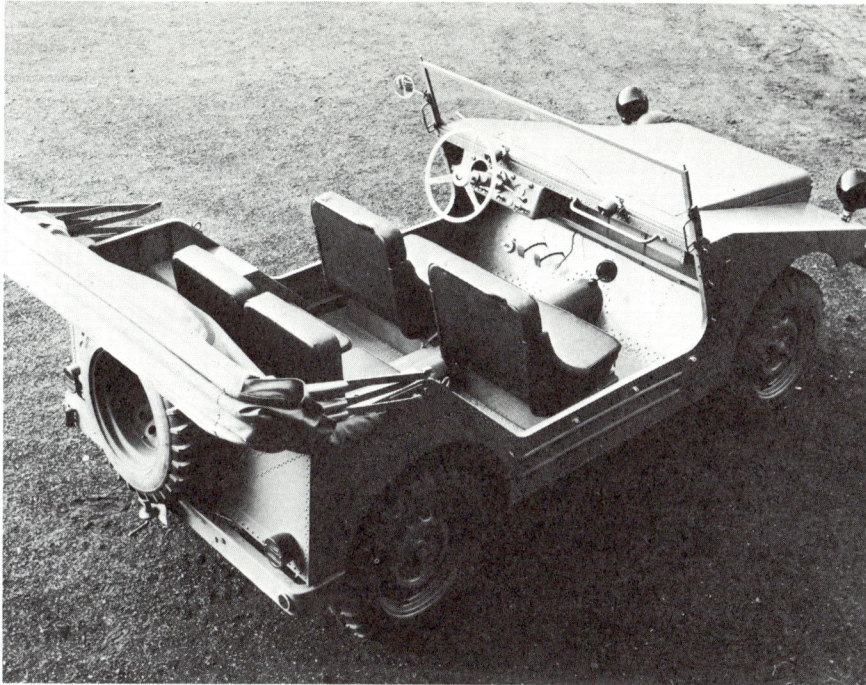

31A Goliath 31

31B Goliath 31

31C Goliath 34/GM1100J

31A: Goliath-Werk GmbH of Bremen, West Germany, produced prototypes for a new field car for the German Bundeswehr in 1954/55, concurrently with Auto Union and Porsche (*q.v.*). They had a ladder-type frame with water-cooled 2-cyl. 2-stroke fuel-injection engine, driving the independently-sprung front wheels. From the rear of the gearbox a propeller shaft drove the conventional leaf-sprung rear axle. In addition to the normal four forward speeds there was a low auxiliary gear (*Geländegang*). The rear-wheel drive could not be disengaged. Most mechanical units were the same as used on contemporary Goliath cars and vans. The bodywork was designed in accordance with *Bundeswehr* specifications and requirements. Shown is one of the first cars, with all-riveted body.

31B: Goliath Model 31 pre-production vehicle under test. There were several pilot models with various detail differences. 50 were ordered by the German Army for extensive trials. These were produced in 1956.

31C: Goliath Model 34/GM1100J *Jagdwagen* soon superseded the Model 31 in production. Major difference was the installation of a 4-stroke engine. This was a water-cooled 50-bhp 1093-cc unit with four horizontally-opposed cylinders as used in the 1957–59 Goliath/Hansa 1100 car and Express 1100 light trucks. It now had eight forward speeds and accelerated from 0–50 mph in 23 seconds. Lowest constant speed was 1·5 mph. Few were made, however, the large government orders having been placed with Auto Union.

HANOMAG, HARRIER

32A Hanomag AL 28A

32B Harrier

32A: **Hanomag** of Hannover-Linden produced relatively large numbers of 1½- and 2½-ton *Allrad* chassis for civilian and military use. In 1963 this 12-seater personnel carrier appeared. It was produced in some quantities for the *Bundesgrenzschutz* (W.-German Border Police) and had a 2·8-litre 70-bhp 4-cyl. diesel engine with 4F1R × 2 transmission. Wheelbase was 3·68 m, length 5·93 m, width 2·06 m, tyre size 10·00-20.

32B: **Harrier** folding car was produced in 1957 by Hunting Percival Aircraft Ltd in Britain, to the design of J. Dolphin. It was a compact lightweight 4-seater which could be air-transported in the form of a box-shaped unit and, after unloading or air-drop, folded out and made ready to go within a few minutes. The rear-mounted power unit was a BSA A10 646-cc twin motorcycle engine of 30 bhp. The vehicle weighed only 700 lb and could reach a top speed of over 60 mph. The gearbox had four forward speeds, no reverse. The British armed forces had at least two: 24AE97 and 26CL15.

32C: **Harrier** in captivity; one of the four prototypes produced for trials and later rejected is now owned by John Couzens, an active member of the All-Wheel Drive Club in Great Britain. One of this Club's main aims is the restoration and preservation of historically interesting military vehicles of all kinds.

32C Harrier

HOTCHKISS JEEP

33A Hotchkiss Jeep M201

33A : **Hotchkiss** and Delahaye, two old-established French car and truck manufacturers, merged in 1954 to form Hotchkiss-Delahaye SA. The new company produced mainly trucks and Jeep vehicles, the latter under Willys licence. Most of the Jeeps were for military use and resembled the wartime Willys MB. All the major parts were interchangeable with wartime Willys MB and Ford GPW, which the French Army also used in large numbers. The French-built Jeep, designated Hotchkiss-Willys M201 VLTT (*Véhicule de Liaison Tout Terrain*), superseded the Delahaye VLR (*q.v.*). Shown is the first Hotchkiss-built Jeep, with a modified radiator grille to accommodate a Sinpar winch.

33B : **Hotchkiss** M201 differed from the 1942–45 Willys MB mainly in having French electrical equipment (24-Volt), carburettor (Solex) and air-cleaner. Engine timing gear used meshed gear wheels (as on Willys CJ3A/MC/M38) instead of a chain and the transmission brake was of the internal expanding type.

33C : **Hotchkiss** produced over 40,000 M201 Jeeps from 1954 until 1969. This picture shows the final assembly line at the Stains plant in 1965. By this time the company name was Hotchkiss-Brandt SA.

33B Hotchkiss Jeep M201

33C Hotchkiss Jeep M201

HOTCHKISS JEEP

34A Hotchkiss Jeep M201

34C Hotchkiss Jeep JH102(D)

34A: **Hotchkiss** M201 in French Army service, 1968. Note windscreen rests located over wipers, rather than on bonnet, and single-piece wheels.

34B: **Hotchkiss** JH101 was first produced in November 1954 and resembled the Willys Jeep Model CJ3B (*q.v.*) except for the engine which was basically the same 60-bhp L-head Four as in the Willys CJ3A (*q.v.*). This was done, obviously, because it was basically the same engine used for the M201. The Willys Jeep CJ3B had the taller 72-bhp Hurricane F-head (inlet-over-exhaust) engine which had necessitated the higher bonnet. Of the JH101 about 3400 were made until 1960.

34C: **Hotchkiss** JH102 superseded the JH101 in January 1961 and was in production until 1970 when Jeep production in France was discontinued. It had 12-Volt electrics, reinforced chassis frame, rear axle and rear springs, lower indirect transfer case ratio (3·82 *v.* 1·97), revised steering, larger fuel tank, different seats and other modifications. Moreover, there was now a diesel engine option; these models were designated JH102D. The vehicle name plates read Hotchkiss-Willys (on radiator grille) and Jeep (below windscreen), but from 1963/64 (when Willys in the USA became Kaiser Jeep) the former was replaced by a Hotchkiss plate.

34D: **Hotchkiss** HWL was a lengthened version of the JH102. With the optional diesel engine it was designated HWLD. The wheelbase was 2·53 m (JH102 : 2·03 m). Tyres were 6·50 instead of 6·00-16. Optional extras included a full-length canvas tilt and rear seats. The JH102D and HWLD had 5·57 instead of 4·875 axle ratios, although early production had 4·48 axles, like the preceding JH101. Shown on the left is a JH102. VIASA, Willys' Spanish licencee, produced virtually identical Jeep vehicles (*see* 39D).

34B
Hotchkiss Jeep JH101

34D Hotchkiss Jeep JH102(D) and HWL(D)

35A International Scout

35B International Scout

35A : International Harvester Co. of Chicago, Illinois, were the first American company to introduce a light 4 × 4 off-road sports utility car to compete with the well-established Willys Jeep models. International's entry into this growing recreational vehicle market was the Scout, which made its public debut in early 1961. During this year over 35,000 were sold which made it the largest selling model in International's truck line. The 100-in wheelbase Scout 4 × 4 had a 152 CID 93-bhp slant-4-cyl. Comanche engine, 3F1R × 2 transmission, separate frame and leaf-sprung live axles. A 4 × 2 version was also available, as were a removable steel cab and a full-length Travel-Top. Soon the range of options expanded with soft-tops (Sport-Tops), winch, PTO, 3-point rear-mounted equipment hitch, flotation tyres, etc. Shown is a 1962 4 × 4 with steel Travel-Top and winch.

35B : International Scout 800B 4 × 4 of 1971. In 10 years of production the Scout had not changed fundamentally but the range of options and accessories had grown. In addition to the economical Four engine (now 196 CID, 111 bhp) there were a 232 CID 145-bhp Six and a 304 CID 193-bhp V8. Transmissions were 3- or 4-speed manual or 3-speed automatic.

35C : International Scout was supplied to the armed forces of several countries, including Australia, Greece (shown) and Yemen. They were also bought by the US Army, Navy and Marine Corps, in 4 × 2 and 4 × 4 form.

35C International Scout

INTERNATIONAL

36A: **International** Scout 800 Sportop, 'the best dressed all-wheel drive car on the road', appeared in 1966 and was supplied with removable hard-top of double-walled fibreglass (shown) or as a convertible with fold-down top of twill. It was available as 4 × 2 or 4 × 4. The spare wheel was mounted on the tail gate. The 152 CID 4-cyl. engine could be supplied with turbo-charger, boosting output from 93·4 to 111·3 bhp. The first Scout was built on 30 November 1960, the 200,000th came off the assembly line on 27 November 1968.

36A International Scout Sportop

36B International Scout II

36B: **International** Scout II made its debut in April 1971 and had completely restyled bodywork. Major features were optional power brakes and steering, air conditioning and luxury trim packages. In addition to the existing Slant-Four, Six and V8 engines (*see* 35B) there was a 197-bhp 345 CID V8. Trac-Lok non-slip differential and three different rear axle ratios were available, in addition to many other options. Shown is the 1973/74 edition, which had vertical instead of horizontal radiator grille bars, and 'silent drive' transfer case. In July 1973 the 300,000th Scout was produced.

36C: **International** 4 × 4 light truck chassis have been in production, with periodical improvements and restyling, for many years. Body styles include pickups, Travelette 4-door 6-seat pickups, Travelall wagons, etc. Various power trains have been and are available. The illustration shows a 1973 C1100 Series Travelall.

36C International C1100

37A : **Isuzu** Motors Ltd of Tokyo, Japan, in 1967 introduced a new 4 × 2 utility vehicle called the Unicab KR80. It had a ladder-type frame with torsion bar independent front suspension and leaf-sprung live rear axle. Many of its mechanical components, including the 58-bhp 1325-cc engine and 4-speed gearbox, were shared with the contemporary Isuzu Bellett passenger car. The engine size was soon increased to 1471 cc (89·8 CID) ; this unit developed 71 bhp and cars thus equipped were designated KR85. Wheelbase was 2·10 m, overall length and width 3·77 × 1·50 m, tyre size 6·00-14, GVW 1500 kg, maximum speed 120 km/h. 1971/72.

37A Isuzu Unicab KR85

37B Isuzu Unicab KR85A

37C Isuzu Unicab KR86A

37D Isuzu Unicab KR86A

37B : **Isuzu** Unicab KR85A 8-seater had higher roof and lengthwise rear seats for six persons. Overall length and most other details were similar to those of the 4-seat KR85.

37C : **Isuzu** Unicab KR86A 4-seater (shown) and KR86B 8-seater appeared in 1973 and had an 84-bhp 1584-cc engine, providing a maximum road speed of 135 km/h. Wheel track, front and rear, was increased by 2 cm to 1·24 and 1·22 m respectively.

37D : **Isuzu** Unicab KR86A front compartment. In spite of its appearance and rugged construction, the Unicab has only rear-wheel drive and consequently a limited off-road performance.

JEEP

38A Jeep CJ2A and CJ3A

38B Jeep CJ3A

38A: Willys-Overland Model CJ2A Universal **Jeep** made its appearance in the summer of 1945 and was a slightly modified version of the famous military 'Truck, $\frac{1}{4}$-ton, 4 × 4, Command Reconnaissance' which the company had been turning out in vast numbers during the war. Main changes were a tail gate, side mounting for the spare wheel, revised top, sealed-beam headlights and steering column gearshift. In 1949/50 the gearshift lever was moved back to the floor and the designation changed to Model CJ3A. The latter also had a single-piece windscreen and several other detail changes. Shown are a CJ2A (left) and a much-modified CJ3A belonging to some Jeep enthusiasts in Gothenburg, Sweden.

38B: Willys-Overland Model CJ3A Universal **Jeep** in its basic form. Unlike the wartime 'Jeep', the 'CJ' had a semi-floating rear axle, an internal expanding drum-type transmission parking brake, revised gear ratios and other modifications.

38C: Willys-Overland Model MC **Jeep** was the military version of the CJ3A and first appeared in 1950. In the US Army it was designated Truck, Utility, $\frac{1}{4}$-ton, 4 × 4, M38. It differed from the CJ3A Universal Jeep mainly in having 24-Volt electrics, provisions for deep-water fording (as shown) and various military fitments such as towing hooks, black-out lighting equipment, etc. In Canada it was assembled for the armed forces by the Ford Motor Co. of Canada (M38CDN). Kits existed for various modifications, e.g. hard-top and winch.

38C Jeep MC/M38

39A Jeep CJ3B

39C Jeep CJ4

39D Jeep VIASA CJ6

39B Jeep CJ3B/M606

39A: **Jeep** CJ3B appeared in 1952, shortly before Willys-Overland was taken over by the Henry J. Kaiser industrial empire, and the name changed to Willys Motors Inc. The CJ3B had a new Hurricane F-head (inlet-over-exhaust valves) engine, based on the existing 134 CID side-valve cylinder block. The new engine's greater height necessitated a higher hood (bonnet) and radiator grille. Of the various overseas production licencees the French (Hotchkiss) and Spanish (VIASA) continued the old engine in the new front end for many years. Shown is the Japanese Mitsubishi-built Model CJ3B-J3R (RHD) which did have the Hurricane engine. This model was available also with a diesel engine, left-hand drive and different body styles (see Mitsubishi). In the USA the old L-head engine was used again for the 4 × 2 DJ3A models which were introduced in 1955.

39B: **Jeep** CJ3B in military livery was designated M606 and supplied to a number of friendly nations under the US Military Assistance Program (MAP). Note black-out driving light on left-hand mudguard and jerrican on right.

39C: **Jeep** CJ4 was produced only in India, by the licence-holders Mahindra & Mahindra Ltd of Bombay. It was a lengthened version of the CJ3B with a wheelbase of 91 instead of 80 in. It was available also as 4 × 2; this model had a tubular front axle and no transfer case. Both were available with enclosed bodywork, named Wagonette. Another India-exclusive was the Jeep FC160 COE (forward-control) with 92-in wheelbase and various body styles.

39D: **Jeep** CJ6 as produced in Spain (VIASA, shown) and France (Hotchkiss, q.v.) was unusual in having the body styling of the CJ3B, the L-head engine of the CJ3A and the wheelbase of the US Jeep CJ6 (q.v.). The Spanish CJ3 was the Model CJ3B with CJ3A engine.

JEEP

40A Jeep CJ5

40A: **Jeep** CJ5 was introduced in 1952, originally in its military guise (M38A1, *q.v.*). It has been in production ever since, albeit with many detail changes and, in recent years, more powerful engines. Shown is a CJ5 with Wagner-Tracs (formerly Uni-Trac) of 1969. This conversion, offered by A. F. Wagner Industries Inc. of Concord, California, included an auxiliary steering system with steering levers actuating the vehicle's left and right wheel brakes. Compared with the CJ3B the CJ5 was 'reskinned' and had 81-in wheelbase. The CJ3B, however, remained in production until 1965 (longer in some foreign countries) as a cheaper Universal model. The restyled CJ5 was also made or assembled in Argentina, Brazil, Canada, Formosa (Taiwan), Italy and several other countries.

40B: **Jeep** CJ5A Tuxedo Park Mark IV of 1964–66 was a luxury and sporty edition of the Universal CJ5, featuring convertible top, chrome bumpers front and rear, wheel embellishers, steering column gearshift and other refinements. In March 1963 the company name Willys Motors Inc. had been changed to Kaiser Jeep Corp.

40B Jeep CJ5A

40C Jeep CJ5

40C: **Jeep** CJ5 and CJ5A were available with Dauntless (ex-Buick) V-6-cyl. engine from 1965. This power unit delivered 160 bhp, compared with the 75 bhp of the standard Hurricane F-head Four. CJ5 shown dates from 1970, the year in which Kaiser Jeep Corp. merged with American Motors Corp. and the company name changed to Jeep Corp. (Subsidiary of AMC). In 4 × 2 from this model was designated DJ5.

40D: **Jeep** CJ5 Renegade of 1974, with V-8-cyl. engine. This engine, as well as two Sixes, had first been introduced by AMC for the 1972 model year. With them came 3- or 4-speed manual and GM Turbo Hydra-Matic transmissions, open-end front axle, wider track, longer (84-in) wheelbase and many other modifications and options. The sporty Renegade was previously available only on a limited basis and featured 'a host of goodies'.

40D Jeep CJ5 Renegade

41A Jeep CJ6A

41A: **Jeep** Universal Model CJ6 was a long-wheelbase (101-in) variant of the standard 81-in CJ5. It had a payload capacity of 1564 lb and was in production from 1955 with the same periodic changes as the CJ5. During 1964–66 there was the 'customized' Model CJ6A Tuxedo Park Mark IV variant (shown) with the same extras as the corresponding Model CJ5A (*q.v.*). The inserted extra body side panel of these long-wheelbase models is just visible in this picture. From 1972 the CJ6 had 104-in wheelbase.

41B: **Jeep** Universal Model 101 was CJ6 chassis with 6-seater 4-door soft-top bodywork produced by Willys-Overland do Brasil SA in 1962. At this time the company produced Aero Willys, Willys, Interlagus and Renault Dauphine and Gordini cars, as well as the Jeep Universal (CJ5), 101 (CJ6), Pickup trucks and Rural Station Wagons (*see* 70A).

41C Jeep CJ6

41C: **Jeep** Universal CJ6 in military service in Switzerland. The Swiss Army also used the CJ5 in militarized form (with military type folding top and other modifications). Other military editions of the CJ5 (in addition to the M38A1, *q.v.*) were the M606A2 and M606A3, which were supplied by the United States under the Military Assistance Program. Military CJ6 Jeep vehicles were also used by the Israeli armed forces.

41B Jeep 101/CJ6

41D Jeep MDA/M170 (pilot)

41D: **Jeep** front line ambulance M170 (Willys, Model MDA) was based on the long-wheelbase CJ6 chassis. This pilot model had different mudguards; production models had the same frontal appearance as the 81-in wheelbase M38A1 (*q.v.*). The MDA was used also for other purposes.

JEEP

42A Jeep MD/M38A1

42A: **Jeep** Truck, ¼-ton, 4 × 4, Utility, M38A1 (Willys MD) was introduced in 1952 and produced in large quantities for the armed forces of the United States and several other countries. Production also took place in Canada (M38A1CDN, assembled by Ford Motor Co. of Canada), the Netherlands ('Nekaf Jeep', assembled by the Nederlandse Kaiser-Frazer-Fabrieken; later by Kemper & Van Twist Diesel), etc. Its civilian counterpart, which became available somewhat later, was the CJ5 (*q.v.*). Basically it was a restyled edition of the M38 Jeep (Willys MC), with 81-in (*v.* 80 in) wheelbase. The power unit was the 72-bhp F-head Hurricane 4-cyl. engine, with 24-Volt electrics and waterproofing equipment. Tyre size was 7·00-16. 1954 model shown.

42B Jeep MD/M38A1

42B: **Jeep** M38A1 with hard-top enclosure and Goodyear 'Terra-tires', one of various experimental modifications.

42C Jeep 'Bobcat'

42C: **Jeep** lightweight vehicle, dubbed 'Bobcat' and 'Aero Jeep' was an experimental model produced by Willys in 1953. It was about 40 inches shorter than the M38A1 and almost 1200 pounds lighter. It had the old L-head 'Go Devil' engine and an aluminium body. After tests by the US Army and Marine Corps it was dropped in favour of the Mighty Mite M422 (*see* American Motors).

42D: **Jeep** M38A1 in captivity. Many Jeeps of various types are now in the hands of private enthusiasts and military vehicle collectors/preservers. This picture was taken at the 1972 Historic Military Vehicle Rally in Shottesbrooke, England.

42D Jeep MD/M38A1

43A Jeep JA-3CB

43B Jeep Utility Wagon

43C Jeep Jeepster

43D Jeep Commando

43A: **Jeep** JA-3CB was a convertible version based on the Willys CJ5 produced by Industrias Kaiser Argentina (IKA) in the late 1950s. It had rear-wheel drive only and a longer body, with removable doors. IKA also produced several other Jeep vehicles, both 4 × 4 and 4 × 2, including the Universal and a Station Wagon (Estanciera).

43B: **Jeep** Utility Wagon of 1961 was available with 4-cyl. Hurricane or 6-cyl. Super Hurricane engine. Wheelbase was 104·5 in, overall dimensions 176¼ × 71¾ × 75¼ in. It was one of a long line of Jeep 4 × 4 Utility vehicles, which included station wagons, pickup trucks, panel vans, etc.

43C: **Jeep** Jeepster models were originally produced by Willys-Overland in the late 1940s (Models VJ2 and VJ3 Phaetons on 104-in wheelbase Station Wagon chassis) and the name was used again for a new series of CJ6-based 4 × 4 models introduced in 1967, comprising Station Wagon, Convertible (shown), Roadster (Commando) and Pickup models. Engine options were the 4-cyl. Hurricane and the Dauntless V6. Wheelbase was 101 in. They were also produced by VIASA in Spain, where all three were known as Commando, with either the Hurricane or a diesel engine.

43D **Jeep** Commando for 1972 had a restyled front, 104-in wheelbase, and was available with 232 CID Six engine (standard) or 258 CID Six or 304 CID V8. The name Jeepster was dropped. Body style availability remained the same (Station Wagon shown.) Discontinued in 1973.

JEEP

44A Jeep Wagoneer

44B Jeep Wagoneer

44C Jeep Wagoneer

44D Jeep Cherokee

44A : **Jeep** Wagoneer 4 × 2 and 4 × 4 J100 Series Station Wagons were announced by Willys Motors in October 1962. They were powered by a 230 CID 6-cyl. OHC engine, named Tornado, driving through a 3-speed manual or automatic transmission. 4 × 4 models had a 2-speed transfer case and overdrive was optional on the 4 × 2 manual. Wheelbase was 110 in, overall length and width $183\frac{1}{2}$ × $75\frac{1}{2}$ in. There were also pickup truck versions, known as Gladiator, and a Panel Delivery van. These models replaced the earlier Utility vehicles (*see* 43B).

44B : **Jeep** Wagoneer from 1973 is available with a new full-time four-wheel drive system, made by Borg-Warner and named Quadra-Trac. It became available also for certain other models in the Jeep range. The Wagoneer's bodywork had remained basically unchanged but the radiator grille had undergone several facelifts.

44C : **Jeep** Wagoneer for 1974 became the marque's top-line model, with restyled radiator grille and, more important, the following features as standard equipment : Quadra-Trac permanent all-wheel drive, 360 CID 2-barrel V8 engine, automatic transmission (GM Hydra-Matic), power steering and front power disc brakes. Lower-priced Jeep Station Wagons were now in the Cherokee series.

44D : **Jeep** Cherokee, new to the line of Jeep vehicles for 1974, is a 109-in wheelbase 2-door sports utility vehicle with integral steel top. The series incorporates a wide range of options, including Quadra-Trac, automatic transmission and V8 engine. Shown is the most luxurious version, the 'S' model. The radiator grille design is similar to that of the Wagoneer of the late 1960s and was also still current on the J10 and J20 Series Jeep Pickup trucks.

45A Kraka 640

45B Kraka

45D Land-Rover

45A: **Kraka** (*Kraftkarren*, power cart), a design of Nicholas Straussler, is an air-transportable multi-purpose vehicle with low-pressure Lypsoid tyres and powered by a rear-mounted 2-cyl. Glas (later BMW) air-cooled engine, driving the rear wheels. Originally the Kraka was made by the Zweirad Union AG of Nuremberg, W. Germany (1962), but later production was taken over by Faun-Werke in nearby Lauf/Pegnitz. The Kraka was sold to military and civilian users and also formed the basis for several variants, incl. a snow-plough (Peter-Mini, Switzerland, 1966). The German *Bundeswehr* uses the Kraka mainly as an equipment and weapon carrier. Shown is the 1973/74 Kraka 640. See also 52B.

45B: The **Kraka** is collapsible to two-thirds of its normal length for ease of air transport and parachuting, as well as for reducing storage space. To do this, the rear end of the vehicle is swivelled underneath, as shown here.

45C: **Lancia** in Italy, in conjunction with Hotchkiss (France) and Büssing (Germany) developed prototypes for a new NATO 0·5-ton 4 × 4 amphibious vehicle. Some were fitted with Lancia flat-4 engines of 1991- and 2086-cc capacity, the latter featuring fuel-injection and torque-converter. Both had 2·10-m wb and a maximum speed of 100 km/h (10·5 in water). 1970/71.

45D: **Land-Rover** was the name given to a cross-country vehicle first made by the Rover Co. Ltd in 1947. The prototype vehicle was a modified war-surplus Willys 'Jeep', fitted with a Rover engine and gearbox.

45E: **Land-Rover** chassis as illustrated in the vehicle's first sales brochure. Clearly visible are the ex-Willys 'Jeep' suspension, (Spicer) axles and transfer case, etc. These were not actually used on production models.

45C Lancia

45E Land-Rover

LAND-ROVER

46A Land-Rover Series I (80) and IIA (88)

46C Land-Rover Series I (86)

46A: Land-Rover made its public debut at the Amsterdam Motor Show in April 1948 and quantity production commenced in the following August in Solihull, England. Shown here is one of these early production models, which became known as the Series I, photographed in 1969 alongside a Series IIA model of 21 years later. The early Land-Rovers had 80-in wheelbase and the contemporary Rover 60 4-cyl. F-head 1595-cc car engine. Transmission was 4F1R × 2 with full-time four-wheel drive. The front-wheel drive was permanently engaged through an over-run free-wheel unit in the transfer case. From 1950 the front-wheel drive could be engaged manually by means of a dog clutch and in 1951 the engine size was increased to 1997-cc. In the British Army the 1595-cc and 1977-cc models were known as the Rover Mk 1 and 2 respectively.

46B: Land-Rover Series I began its military career with the British Army in 1949 and first saw active service in Korea in 1950–52 where it had to 'compete' with the American 'Jeep' of Second World War fame. The Rover product scored on account of its better weather protection but needed much development work. Illustrated is a survivor of one of the earliest batches delivered to the British Army, next to a modern ½-ton military version (Rover I) in the early 1970s.

46C: Land-Rover Series I of the Australian Army, riding high on two steel wires. For this purpose flanged hubs were attached to the wheels. Vehicle shown had 86-in wheelbase, an increase of 6 in. Commonly known as the '86-inch' this model was in production from August 1953 and in the British Army it was designated Rover Mk 3. In June 1956 the wheelbase was increased to 88 in for the Regular (as opposed to 107-in wb Long models) and from June 1957 a 2-litre diesel engine was available.

46B Land-Rover Series I (80) and Rover I

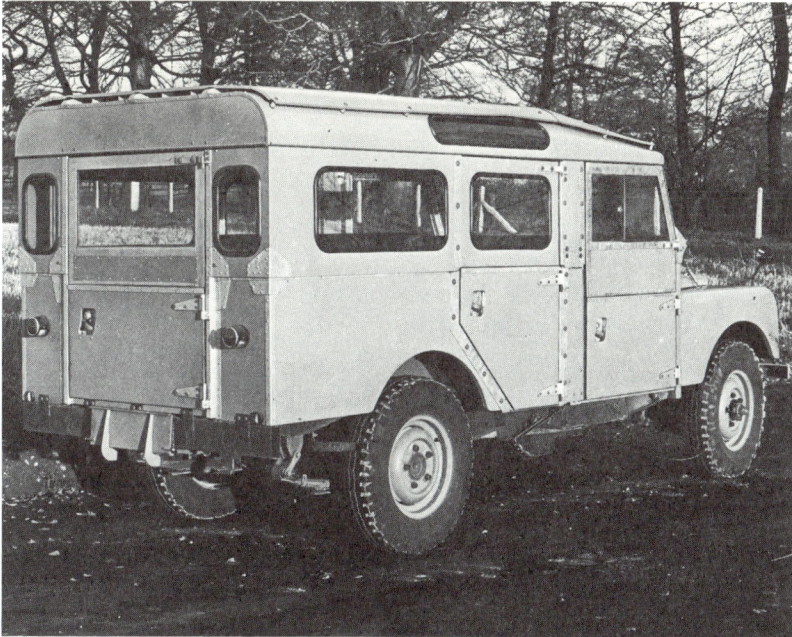

47A Land-Rover Series I (107)

47B Land-Rover Series II (88)

47C Land-Rover Series IIA (88)

47A : **Land-Rover** Series I Long 10-seater Station Wagon was introduced in November 1955. It had a 107-in wheelbase, which from August 1953 had been used for a Pickup truck. This Station Wagon was discontinued in November 1958, when it was superseded by the Series II with 109-in wheelbase.

47B : **Land-Rover** Series II Regular models were announced in February 1958 and were available with petrol or diesel engine. Wheelbase remained 88-in but track width was increased from 50 to $51\frac{1}{2}$ in. Modifications included revised body styling with sills below the doors, relocation of fuel filler from under driver's seat to side of body, improved suspension, etc. In March 1958 a new Series II 109-in wheelbase Pickup was introduced, the new $2\frac{1}{4}$-litre petrol engine of which was fitted to the Series II Regular and 2-door Station Wagon from the following August. Shown is a Series II Regular with hard-top, coupled to a Scottorn Bushmaster powered-axle trailer of 1960. The trailer axle was driven from the vehicle's PTO.

47C : **Land-Rover** Series IIA first appeared in September 1961 and had only minor modifications. Major feature was the introduction of a new (optional) $2\frac{1}{4}$-litre diesel engine. Illustrated is a Series IIA petrol-engined Regular model of the British Army, where it was known as the Rover 8. From 1955 the Land-Rover was the British Army's standard $\frac{1}{4}$-ton 4 × 4 forward area vehicle, supplanting the Austin Champ (*q.v.*). These military versions had only relatively minor modifications to meet military requirements, until the late 1960s when a new type, the $\frac{1}{2}$-ton Rover I (*q.v.*), was introduced as the new standard military 4 × 4 utility vehicle.

LAND-ROVER

48A Land-Rover Series IIA (88)

48B Land-Rover Series II (88)/Cuthbertson

48C Land-Rover Series II (88)

48D Land-Rover Series III (109)

48A : **Land-Rover** vehicles were frequently modified for special purposes, both by civilian and military operators. This Series IIA of the British Military Police is one of several 'customized' models used for the conveyance of VIPs at parades and other official events. They are also known as Royal Escort Land-Rovers.

48B : **Land-Rover** with Cuthbertson four-track conversion kit. The standard wheels were replaced by sprockets which drove the four-track bogies, each with four pneumatic-tyred wheels. A few of these were used in the 1960s, mainly by bomb disposal squads. Steering was, not surprisingly, power-assisted.

48C : **Land-Rover** vehicles are exported to many countries, for civilian, military and other users. Shown is a Series II 88 in Australian Army service. Assembled locally, these models had different front wing cut-outs and no sills below the doors. Note the hefty brush guard at the front.

48D : **Land-Rover** Series III was officially launched on 1 October 1971. It is outwardly identified by a restyled radiator grille and badge and furthermore incorporates a redesigned safety fascia (with the instrument panel moved from the centre to the driver's side), an all-synchromesh gearbox and many detail improvements. By this time some 850,000 Land-Rovers had been produced, over 75% of which were for export to more than 180 overseas markets. The headlamps were mounted in the front wings from 1969 (models for Benelux countries from 1968). Shown is a 109 4-door 12-seater Station Wagon of 1974.

49A: **Land-Rover** ½-ton 4 × 4 Lightweight model made its debut in 1966. It was an experimentally modified Series IIA with standard 88-in wheelbase, reduced width and completely redesigned bodywork, developed for ease of air transport, air-drops and lifting by helicopter. It weighed about 3100 lb in stripped-down form. Vehicle shown took part in the British Army's 'Operation Wagon Trail' in 1967.

49B: **Land-Rover** ½-ton (Rover I) production model in stripped-down form. From 1971 the headlamps, side lights and direction indicator lights were mounted in forward extensions of the front wings. The ½-ton is available in both 12-Volt Cargo and 24-Volt FFR (fitted for radio) versions. The latter has two instead of three front seats, the centre space being occupied by two 12-Volt batteries. The Cargo version weighs 3210 lb (1456 kg), or 2660 lb (1206 kg) in stripped-down form. GVW is about 4450 lb (2018 kg). In 1971 the Land-Rover in its various forms was standardized, or in service, with military or para-military forces of some 140 territories overseas.

49C: **Land-Rover** ½-ton, known in the British Army as the Rover I, in its initial production form. Mechanically it was similar in most respects to the Army's Rovers Mk 8 and 10, which it superseded. It is shown here with front-mounted winch and full weather protection installed. A hard-top was fitted on certain models. 1969/70.

49B Land-Rover ½-ton

49A Land-Rover ½-ton

49C Land-Rover ½-ton

MBB, MINERVA

50A MBB 0·5 t

50B MBB 0·5 t

50C: **Minerva** of Mortsel, Antwerp, Belgium, licence-produced the Land-Rover in the early 1950s, chiefly for the Belgian armed forces and these vehicles remained in service for more than 20 years. They differed from the British Land-Rover (80-in wb Series I) mainly in having reshaped front mudguards and radiator grille. Spare wheel and jerrican were carried on the back. Belgian-assembled Willys CJ3A Jeeps were used also.

50D: **Minerva** 86-in wb *Tout Terrain* prototype was introduced in 1954, when Land-Rover production came to an end. It was offered as 6- or 9-seater, with Continental petrol or Jenbach diesel engine. Production models were designated C20 (later C22) and M20 (civilian and military resp.) but few were produced.

50E: **Minerva** C20 (shown), C22 and M20 had monocoque construction with engine and transmission mounted on an easily removable subframe, as illustrated (Continental engine).

50A: **MBB** amphibious 4 × 4 cross-country vehicle for a payload of 0·5 ton was developed by Messerschmitt-Bölkow-Blohm GmbH of Ottobrunn, W. Germany, in conjunction with the Federal Office of Military Technology and Procurement and the Ministry of Defence. It made its debut, in prototype form, in 1971, with a 95-bhp BMW 4-cyl. engine. In 1972 a second prototype appeared, powered by a centrally-mounted 70-bhp MAN L9204 multi-fuel engine.

50B: The **MBB** had a fibreglass reinforced plastic hollow body with polyurethane hard foam core. This fibreglass sandwich construction, developed by MBB in conjunction with the Bayer concern, is self-supporting (rather than having merely a shaping function) and yet is much lighter than a sheet metal hull.

50C Minerva/Land-Rover

50D Minerva *Tout Terrain*

50E Minerva C20

51A Mitsubishi Jeep J20(D)

51B Mitsubishi Jeep J21(D)C

51C Mitsubishi Jeep J32(D)

51D Mitsubishi Jeep J30(D)

51A: **Mitsubishi** Heavy Industries Ltd (later Mitsubishi Motor Corp.) of Japan entered into a licence-production agreement with Willys (later Kaiser Jeep) of the USA in 1953 and from that time have produced a wide range of Jeep vehicles for military and civilian use. Shown on this page are some models which differed in major respects from the US models. These were all developed from the basic Willys CJ3B Universal Jeep [which was also manufactured by Mitsubishi, designated J3 (see 39A) ; variants were the JC3 Diesel and their RHD variants J3R and J3RD]. Shown is the basic model of the J20 Series as offered during the 1960s. It had 2·225-m (88-in) wb, special 7-seater bodywork, steel front doors with winding windows and double rear doors. Engine was JH4 Hurricane F-head (76-bhp) or KE31 diesel (61 bhp), both 134·2 CID ($3\frac{1}{8} \times 4\frac{3}{8}$ in) Fours. Gear shift lever was steering column-mounted on RHD models.

51B: **Mitsubishi Jeep** Model J21C and J21DC (Diesel) were metal-top versions in the J20 Series. With RHD their designations were J20C and J20DC respectively. Note the forward extensions to the front wings which was not unlike the US Jeep CJ5 (q.v.).

51C: **Mitsubishi Jeep** Model J32 and J32D (Diesel) had 2·64-m (104-in) wheelbase and seating for 9. It was available only with right-hand drive. 1968 model shown.

51D: **Mitsubishi Jeep** Model J30 and J30D (Diesel) were mechanically similar to J32 and J32D but with all-steel station wagon bodywork and less austere finish. Called Delivery Wagon they carried up to six adults with 250 kg of cargo or three adults plus 400 kg.

MOSKVITCH, MV, NISSAN

52A: **Moskvitch** 410 was a 4 × 4 cross-country version of the Soviet Moskvitch 402 4-door 4-seater passenger car, produced during 1956–58 (with 35-bhp 1220-cc engine) and 1958–60 (Model 410N with 45-bhp 1360-cc engine). Transmission comprised a 3-speed gearbox with 2-speed transfer case. Wheelbase was 2·38 m, track 1·22 m, front and rear.

52A Moskvitch 410(N)

52B MV Agusta Diana

52B: **MV** Agusta (Meccanica Verghera), the well-known motorcycle manufacturers of Gallarate, Italy, produced the German Kraka (q.v.) under licence and in addition to the Lypsoid-tyred basic folding model offered this hard-top variant, known as Diana, in the mid-1960s. Like the Kraka, it had the driver's seat centrally at front, but up to 6 passengers could sit on lengthwise bench seats in the open-sided cabin. The vehicle measured 3·20 × 1·60 × 1·76 m.

52C: **Nissan** Patrol Model 4W60 of the early 1950s closely followed the lines of the wartime US 'Jeep' but had a 3670-cc (224 CID) 85-bhp 6-cyl. side-valve petrol engine, 4-speed gearbox with single-speed transfer case and right-hand drive. Wheelbase was 2·20 m (86·5 in). It was offered also as chassis/cowl for special bodywork, e.g. fire-fighting trucks.

52C Nissan Patrol 4W60

52D: **Nissan** Patrol 4W65 Station Wagon of about 1959 had all-steel bodywork, seating 8 persons, all facing forward. It had a wheelbase of 2·51 m and was 4·27 m long. Weight was 1780 kg, tyre size 6·50-16. The engine was a 3956-cc 105-bhp Six, driving the live axles through a 4F1R × 2 transmission.

52D Nissan Patrol 4W65

53A Nissan Patrol L60

53B Nissan Patrol L60

53C Nissan Patrol Station Wagon (SWB)

53D Nissan Patrol Station Wagon (LWB)

53A: **Nissan** Patrol in its basic form as produced throughout the 1960s and early 1970s with periodical detail changes and improvements. It had a 3956-cc (242 CID) OHV Six engine with a gross output of 135 bhp (later increased to 145 bhp), driving through a 3-speed gearbox with 2-speed transfer case. The Patrol has a welded box-section ladder-type frame with leaf-sprung live axles. Standard wheelbase size was 2·20 m, track front 1·38 m, rear 1·40 m.

53B: **Nissan** Patrol Model L60 of 1972. The RHD version was designated Model 60 or 60U. In addition to the 6-seater (L)60 with standard wheelbase size (shown) there was the (L)G60 with 2·50-m wheelbase which provided seating for 8 persons and was 70 kg heavier, at 1640 kg. There was also a fire-fighting version on the 2·50-m wheelbase chassis (Model F(L)G60). In India the Nissan Patrol was licence-produced under the name Jonga.

53C: **Nissan** Patrol Station Wagons have been available with 2·20-, 2·50- and 2·80-m wheelbase. Shown is a short-wheelbase 2-door wagon with optional front-mounted winch. It looked rather similar to the Model K60 Hard-top version of the basic (L)60 vehicle.

53D: **Nissan** Patrol long-wheelbase 4-door Station Wagon of the early 1970s, destined for the Consulate General of Japan in Madras, India. All Patrols except 4 × 2 models (which were also available) had Tracta type constant velocity joints in the front axle.

54A Nuffield FV1800

54A : **Nuffield** Mechanizations Ltd produced three pilot models for a post-war British replacement for the US 'Jeep'. Work on this project had started during the war, under the direction of Mr (later Sir) Alec Issigonis. Seen here during a test run at Chobham is the first prototype. It featured a stressed-skin welded steel body and torsion bar independent suspension front and rear. The power unit was a horizontally-opposed 4-cyl. L-head petrol unit. The projected vehicle was designated Car, 5-cwt, 4 × 4, FV 1800 Series.

54B : **Nuffield** prototype No. 2 (No. 3 carried registration number JLR491 ; both were issued in London in late 1947) differed from the original in having bolted-on mudguards, vertical slots in the front panel and other details. This vehicle, dubbed 'Gutty', has been preserved.

54B Nuffield FV1800 'Gutty'

54C Nuffield/Wolseley FV1800 'Mudlark'

54C : **Nuffield** FV1800 Series, pre-production model. A few of these cars were made at Nuffield's Wolseley works at Ward End, Birmingham, in 1949. They were also known as Wolseley GP Vehicle, 5-cwt, 4 × 4, or 'Mudlark'. In addition to a completely restyled body, these cars had a newly standardized Rolls-Royce 4-cyl. engine, driving through a 5-speed gearbox. After further modifications the vehicle was taken into quantity production by the Austin Motor Co. (*q.v.*) in 1952.

55A Opel Blitz

55B OSI Cross Country 124

55A : Opel Blitz 9-seater of 1956 was a prototype produced for the German *Bundeswehr*. It had three bench seats (two facing each other in the rear compartment) and a large locker. Opel also produced a light truck on the same chassis (*Lkw 0,75 t gl*). The company did not have sufficient spare capacity for mass production, however, and the Borgward B2000A/O (*q.v.*), which was similar in general configuration, was adopted by the new German Federal Army as the standard vehicle of this type. The Opel had a wheelbase of 3·30 m, leaf-sprung live axles, 9·00-16 tyres and a 2·5-litre OHV Six engine of 71 bhp with 4F1R × 2 transmission.

55B : OSI Cross-Country 124 of 1966 was based on the Fiat 124 car. It was a 4 × 2 equipped with a reduction gear and a lockable differential.

Doors and bonnet were made of reinforced polyester resin. Engine timing system and carburation were modified for better low speed performance. OSI (of Turin) also designed a field car based on the smaller Fiat 850.

55C : P2 was the designation of a 4-seater 4 × 4 field car produced during the late 1950s in Zwickau, East Germany. There were two versions, the P2M '*Kübel*' (shown) and the P2S *Schwimmwagen* (amphibious car). Both had a 65-bhp 6-cyl. engine of 2407 cc with 4F1R × 2 transmission.

55D : P3 was the successor of the P2M and provided seating for 7. It appeared in 1962 and was a much improved vehicle. Like the P2M it had independent suspension with torsion bars. Engine power was increased to 75 bhp. It became the standard military field car in the German Democratic Republic (DDR).

55C P2M

55D P3

56A Peking BJ212

56A: **Peking** BJ212 4-door field car, also
known as 'War Horse', was launched in the
mid-1960s in the People's Republic of China.
The picture shows Chairman Mao Tse-Tung in
an early production model in 1967. The car is
powered by a 4-cyl. OHV engine of 2445 cc
(92 × 92 mm) with 6·6:1 CR and an output of
75 bhp at 3500–4000 rpm. Transmission
comprises a 3-speed gearbox with high and
low range, driving live axles with semi-elliptic
leaf springs. Tyre size is 6·50-16, wheelbase
2·30 m. The vehicle weighs 1530 kg (fully
loaded 1955 kg) and has a speed range of
3–98 km/h. A 2-door truck version is also
made. Several other field cars have appeared in
Red China but few have been produced in
quantity.

56B: **Peugeot** produced several experimental
field cars, starting in 1950 with the Model
203R. It was followed by the improved 203RA
(shown). Two of each were made as prototypes
for the French Army but the Delahaye *VLR*
(*q.v.*) was adopted instead.
56C: **Peugeot** 203RA used a modified Peugeot
203 passenger car engine, an 8CV OHV Four
of 64 bhp (Model 203R had the standard 7CV
1290-cc 48·5-bhp engine). It had a 4-speed
gearbox (overdrive top) with 2-speed transfer
and 3·40-m wb.
56D: **Peugeot** 403RB appeared in 1955. It
was powered by the 403 8CV 64-bhp engine.
The bonnet was forward-hinged as on the
Delahaye *VLR*. Only 12 were made. All these
VSPs (*Véhicule Spéciale Peugeot*) had live
axles with leaf springs.

56B Peugeot 203RA

56C Peugeot 203RA

56D Peugeot 403RB

57A: **Plymouth** Trail Duster made its debut in January 1974 and was identical in most respects to the Dodge Ramcharger (q.v.). Both are products of the Chrysler Corporation in the USA and are full-time four-wheel drive sports utility vehicles, the market for which has shown a steady growth in recent years. It is shown here with optional roll bar and front and rear passenger seats.

57B: **Plymouth** Trail Duster with optional high-line Sport Package, including luxurious interior and exterior trim items and metal roof. Alternative optional roof is a folding canvas type. Standard tyres are E78 × 15/B, 4-ply rating; there are 11 other tyre options, both car and truck types.

57B Plymouth Trail Duster

57A Plymouth Trail Duster

57C: **Porsche**, like Auto Union and Goliath (q.v.) produced prototypes for a new field car for the German *Bundeswehr* in 1954/55. Shown is the 1954 pilot model during off-road trials. It had a Porsche flat-4 car engine, mounted in the tail of a monocoque body, four-wheel drive and independent suspension.

57D: **Porsche** Model 597 of 1955 and later had strengthening ribs pressed in the body panels. Relatively few were produced since military orders were not forthcoming. The final production models (1957/58) had four-door bodywork. Most went to civilian customers and surviving models are now collector's items.

57C Porsche

57D Porsche 597

58A Renault 500 kg 4 × 4

58C Renault R2087

58D: **Renault** 4 and 6 Rodéo of 1974 are based on the Renault front-wheel drive Models 4 and 6 passenger cars respectively. Of both there are three versions: *Évasion* (entirely open), *Chantier* (covered driving compartment), *Coursière* (full-length soft-top) and *Quatre Saisons* (fully enclosed with black top, doors with sliding windows, as shown in foreground). The Rodéo was originally offered by ACL of Arlanc on the Renault 4 chassis. The 4 and the 6 have 4-cyl. engines of 845 and 1108 cc respectively, driving the front wheels through a 4-speed gearbox. Both are available with additional rear-wheel drive (4 × 4 conversion by Sinpar). Wheelbase is 2·40 m on the left-hand side, 48 mm more on the right. The difference is caused by the fact that the full-width torsion bars of the rear suspension trailing arms lay one behind the other.

58B Renault 500 kg 4 × 4

58A: **Renault** 500 kg 4 × 4 *Tous Terrains* chassis with 2·66-m wheelbase, 2-litre (85 × 88 mm) 52-bhp 4-cyl. engine and 4F1R × 2 transmission was available in the early 1950s. It was basically the contemporary Colorale chassis, converted to four-wheel drive. Gradeability was 55%.

58B: **Renault** 500 kg 4 × 4 *Tous Terrains* with *Break* (station wagon) bodywork of 1952. Other body styles included pickup and van.

58C: **Renault** Model R2087 4 × 4 light truck chassis with personnel carrier/command car bodywork of 1953.

58D Renault/ACL Rodéo

59A : **Renault** front-wheel drive cars and vans of various types have been converted to four wheel drive by the firm of Sinpar in Colombes near Paris since 1964. The conversion consists of a power take-off at the forward end of the front-mounted gearbox, a propeller shaft to a rear differential unit, drive shafts to the rear wheels, modified suspension arms, brakes, etc. Shown is the 845-cc prototype of 1964.

59B : **Renault** 4 with Sinpar 4 × 4 conversion; underneath view showing the drive line as used in 1966. On later models there were detail modifications and improvements but the general configuration remained the same. The car's original final drive ratio of 8 × 33 was changed to 6 × 28. Rear-wheel drive could be disengaged by means of a lever under the dashboard.

59C : **Renault** 6 *Berline* and Rodéo (*q.v.*) can also be converted by Sinpar. In addition to standard-bodied Renault cars and vans, Sinpar offer a *Torpédo* (military type soft-top conversion of R4 van), a *Torpédo S* (re-bodied, square styling), a pickup truck, etc. All have Renault's optional heavy-duty suspension.

59A Renault/Sinpar R4

59B Renault/Sinpar R4

59C Renault/Sinpar R6

ROVER

60A Range Rover

60B Range Rover

60A **Rover** introduced the Range Rover on 17 June 1970 as their entry into the fast-growing 'leisure market'. Rather than a glorified Land-Rover (*q.v.*) the Range Rover was an entirely new concept, combining the features of a luxury station wagon with those of a heavy-duty multi-purpose vehicle. Its 3·5-litre 130-bhp engine (a light-alloy modified Buick V8), combined with excellent handling characteristics and permanent all-wheel drive, provides a safe high-speed cruising ability and its transmission system, comprising a 4-speed gearbox, 2-speed transfer case and lockable centre differential, gives excellent cross-country performance and maximum tractability on slippery roads. Wheelbase is 100 in, overall length and width 176 × 70 in.

60B : **Rover** Range Rover military version was first shown in October 1970 as a private venture but military interest was nothing compared with that of other government services such as the police, ambulance and fire brigades. Longer wheelbase and 6-wheeled conversions (by outside firms) soon appeared for the latter two applications.

60C : **Rover** Range Rovers, suitably modified and equipped, were used in the gruelling British Army-led Trans-American Expedition which took place in late 1971/early 1972. The route led from Alaska to Cape Horn and included crossing the infamous Darien Gap and the Atrato Swamp, which were the last geographical barriers in the way of a plan to link North and South America by road.

60C Range Rover

60D Range Rover

60D : **Rover** Range Rover chassis, showing (1) third diff, (2) coil-sprung live axles, (3) self-levelling unit, (4) disc brakes all round, (5) dual-line front brake piping, (6) brake servo, (7) parking brake, (8) 4F1R all-synchromesh gearbox, (9) radial-ply tyres, (10) collapsible steering column, (11) 19-Imp. gal. fuel tank, (12) impact absorbing fascia.

61A : **SAIPAC**, the Teheran Citroën producers, launched this Dyane-based 'Bush Baby' about 1970, as an Iranian variety of the Citroën Mehari (*q.v.*). A similar car is built in Saigon, Vietnam, called Dalat. Both have sheet metal bodywork.

61A SAIPAC 'Bush Baby'

61B Savio Jungla 600

61B : **Savio** Jungla 600, a light 4-seater 4 × 2 field car introduced in 1966 by the Turin firm of Giuseppe Savio, was based on components of the Fiat 600D car and had 2·00-m wb, 5·20-14 tyres and 32-bhp (gross) rear engine with 4-speed gearbox. Overall length and width were 3·21 × 1·35 m. A larger model with four doors, the Savana, based on the Fiat 124, also appeared in 1966, followed by the Fiat 500-based Albarella, in 1967. Only the Jungla 600, however, was produced in quantity—originally in Italy and more recently in conjunction with SEAT, the Spanish Fiat licencee.

61C : **Scania-Vabis**, for many years Sweden's distributors of US Willys Jeep vehicles, in the late 1950s built two experimental ¾-ton 4 × 4 military vehicles, based on the contemporary Jeep FC170 chassis. Owing to the Swedish Army's acceptance of the Volvo Laplander (*q.v.*) the project was shelved.

61D : **Scoiattolo** (squirrel) was the name of some Italian cars introduced in 1969 by Carrozzeria Arrigo Perini (CAP) of Arco, Trento. There was a 4 × 2 model, based on Fiat 500 mechanical components, and a 4 × 4 4-seater, the Super Scoiattolo, which had Fiat 600 running gear and is shown here. It had a speed range of 2·5—90 km/h, 5·60-12 tyres and many optional extras. Other Fiat-based 'fun cars' include the 4 × 2 front-drive Scout 127, made by the coachbuilding firm of Fissore, and Moretti's Mini- and Midimaxi with Fiat 500 and 127 units respectively, all of which appeared in 1970/71.

61E : **Siva** Llama, a British multi-purpose car with fibreglass body designed in 1973 and based on Chrysler Imp mechanical components. Wheelbase is 81 in, length 136 in, width 57 in, weight 1200 lb, speed 80 mph. Siva had previously offered the Mule, a similar-looking car in DIY kit-form.

61C Scania-Vabis/Willys FC170

61D Scoiattolo (CAP)

61E Siva Llama

SKODA, SKOPAK, STEYR-PUCH

62A Skoda 1100VO

62B Skoda 973P

62C Skopak

62A: **Skoda** 1100VO was a 4 × 2 command car produced for the Czechoslovakian Army during the late 1940s. Based on the contemporary Skoda 1100 passenger car it had independent suspension with transversal leaf springs. A similar type was produced by Tatra (q.v.). Both were eventually superseded by the Soviet GAZ-69A (q.v.) and many ended up in Civvy Street, as shown. It also appeared with four-wheel drive; this was a proper cross-country vehicle but never got beyond the prototype stage.

62B: **Skoda** 973P, a 4 × 4 vehicle of which a few were made in 1952. It had independent suspension with longitudinal torsion bars, and 7·50-16 tyres. The 35-bhp 1221-cc OHV Four engine drove through a 4F1R × 2 transmission and wheel hub reduction gears. Another limited-production 4 × 4 Skoda was the Model 997Z Universal of 1964, which resembled the Steyr-Puch Haflinger (q.v.) in appearance.

62C: **Skopak** is a Pakistan-built utility car based on the Skoda Octavia Combi 2·40-m wheelbase chassis and was introduced in 1970 by Haroon Industries Ltd (later Republic Motors Ltd) of Karachi. It measures 4·20 × 1·64 m. The bodywork comprises plastic panels on a steel frame.

62D: **Steyr-Puch** Haflinger 4 × 4 lightweight multi-purpose vehicle has been in production since 1959. Named after a famous breed of Austrian horse it has been supplied for civilian and military use in various countries. The basic vehicle is an open platform type. Various types of superstructures are available, including a closed cab.

62E: **Steyr-Puch** Haflinger 700AP chassis, three-quarter rear view. Engine (flat-twin), gearbox (4F1R, later models 5F1R) and lockable differentials are built en-bloc with the chassis backbone tube.

62F: **Steyr-Puch** Haflinger in service with the Australian Army. Folding rear seats are optional. The vehicle is ideally suited for air-drops by parachute and for transport by helicopter.

62D Steyr-Puch Haflinger

62E Steyr-Puch Haflinger

62F Steyr-Puch Haflinger

63A Steyr-Puch Pinzgauer 710

63B Steyr-Puch Pinzgauer 710

63C Suzuki LJ10 Jimny

63A: **Steyr-Puch** Pinzgauer 710, bigger brother of the Haflinger, was first announced in 1965 and made its public debut in Graz, Austria, on 17 May 1971. Like the Haflinger it is named after a well-known Austrian work horse. In 1968 a 6 × 6 version (Model 712) was designed. By 1971 both types were in production for the Austrian and Swiss armed forces, and from 1972/73 they have been available commercially.

63B: **Steyr-Puch** Pinzgauer 710 chassis is similar in principle to that of the Haflinger but the engine, a 2·5-litre air-cooled horizontal 4-cyl. in-line unit, developing 87—90 bhp at 4000 rpm, is placed above the front wheel axis. Transmission comprises a 5F1R main gearbox with 2-speed auxiliary gearbox. Both axles have diff locks. Wheelbase is 2·20 m.

63C: **Suzuki** LJ10 Jimny from Japan is one of the world's smallest 4 × 4 vehicles. Weighing only 630 kg, it measures 3·00 × 1·30 m. It is propelled by an air-cooled 27-bhp 2-cyl. 2-stroke engine of 359 cc and has a 4F1R × 2 transmission, leaf-sprung live axles and 6·00-16 tyres. Max. road speed is 80 km/h, wheelbase 1·93 m. Picture was taken in Australia in 1972. 1973/4 model (LJ20) has vertical slats in radiator grille.

63D: **Tatra** in Czechoslovakia continued production of the wartime T57K (shown) for a short while. It was a 4 × 2 *Kübelwagen*, derived from the T57a car with air-cooled flat-4 engine and tubular backbone chassis.

63E: **Tatra** 801 was one of an interesting series of experimental 4 × 4 vehicles made in the early 1950s. As can be seen, it was an amphibian, shaped much like the US amphibious 'Jeep'. It was, however, more sophisticated, featuring independent suspension and a rear-mounted air-cooled engine (Tatra 900 4-cyl., 2438 cc, 55 bhp at 3200 rpm).

63F: **Tatra** 803, another prototype, was a four-door field car with 2545-cc air-cooled V8 engine. Like the T801 it had independent suspension with swing axles. The only vehicle in the T800 Series to reach the production stage was the T805, a light COE truck.

63D Tatra 57K

63E Tatra 801

63F Tatra 803

TEMPO/LAND-ROVER, TOYOTA

64A Tempo/Land-Rover 041

64A: **Tempo** 041 was licence-produced Land-Rover (*q.v.*) with German bodywork, supplied to the *Bundesgrenzschutz* (German Border Police). Shown is the 1954 edition with 2·18-m wheelbase; earlier models (1952/53) had 2·03-m wheelbase, corresponding with the British Land-Rover 86 and 80 respectively.

64B: **Toyota** of Japan introduced their first ¼-ton 4 × 4, Model BJ, in the early 1950s. Like the early Nissan Patrol (*q.v.*), it was powered by a 6-cyl. truck engine, driving through a 4-speed gearbox with single-speed transfer case. The Toyota's engine was a 3386-cc OHV unit of 82–85 bhp, rather similar to the US Chevrolet 'Stovebolt Six'. Wheelbase of the Model BJ was 2·40 m, overall length 3·79 m. From the rear it was hardly distinguishable from the US 'Jeep', on which the vehicle was clearly patterned. In addition to the type shown there was a version with doors, tail gate, rear quarter side curtains and spare wheel located on the left of the cowl (with fender well). It was also available with special fire-fighting bodywork and equipment.

64B Toyota BJ

64C: **Toyota** Land Cruiser of the late 1950s had been completely restyled and became a serious contender in the world's markets for ¼-ton 4 × 4 vehicles. It now had an even more powerful engine (3878-cc, 105 bhp, later 120, 135, 145 and eventually 155 bhp, gross). Model FJ25 shown dates from about 1960, at which time there were two wheelbase sizes and a variety of body styles.

64C Toyota Land Cruiser FJ25

64D: **Toyota** Land Cruiser Model FJ28 Station Wagon of 1959/60 was built on the long-wheelbase chassis (2·43 m; standard models 2·28 m). It measured 4·36 × 1·69 m, seated five and had a max. road speed of 110 km/h.

64D Toyota Land Cruiser FJ28

65A Toyota Land Cruiser FJ45V

65B Toyota Land Cruiser FJ55V

65A: **Toyota** Land Cruiser range was developed further during the 1960s and the 4F1R × 1 transmission was replaced by the more suitable 3F1R × 2 system. All models had rugged ladder-type chassis frames with leaf-sprung live axles and a wide range of optional equipment and accessories was available. Illustrated is a Model FJ45V 4-door Station Wagon of the mid-1960s. It had a wheelbase of 2·65 m and 7·00-15 tyres. Other Land Cruiser wheelbase sizes were 2·28 m (FJ40 soft- and hard-top models), 2·43 m (FJ43 soft-top) and 2·95 m (FJ45P-B truck).

65B: **Toyota** Land Cruiser 4-door Station Wagon was completely restyled for the 1968 model year. It was designated Model FJ55V and

had a wheelbase of 2·70 m. Overall length and width were 4·67 × 1·73 m. Engine output was 145 bhp (gross; 155 bhp from 1970). Tyre size was 7·00-15. Other Land Cruiser models retained the earlier front end styling.

65C: **Toyota** Land Cruisers are also made in Brazil, where Toyota do Brasil SA of São Paulo in the late 1960s offered the four variants shown here. Known as the Toyota Bandeirante series they are, from left to right: Model OJ40LV-B 7-seat wagon (wheelbase 2·75 m), Model OJ40L soft-top (wb 2·28), Model OJ40LV hard-top (wb 2·28) and Model OJ45 LP-B 1-ton truck (wb 2·95 m). All are powered by a 4-cyl. Mercedes-Benz OM324 diesel engine of 78 bhp (gross).

65C Toyota Bandeirante OJ40/45 Series

TRABANT, TREKKA, TRIUMPH, UAZ

66A Trabant P601/A

66C Triumph Pony

66D UAZ-469B

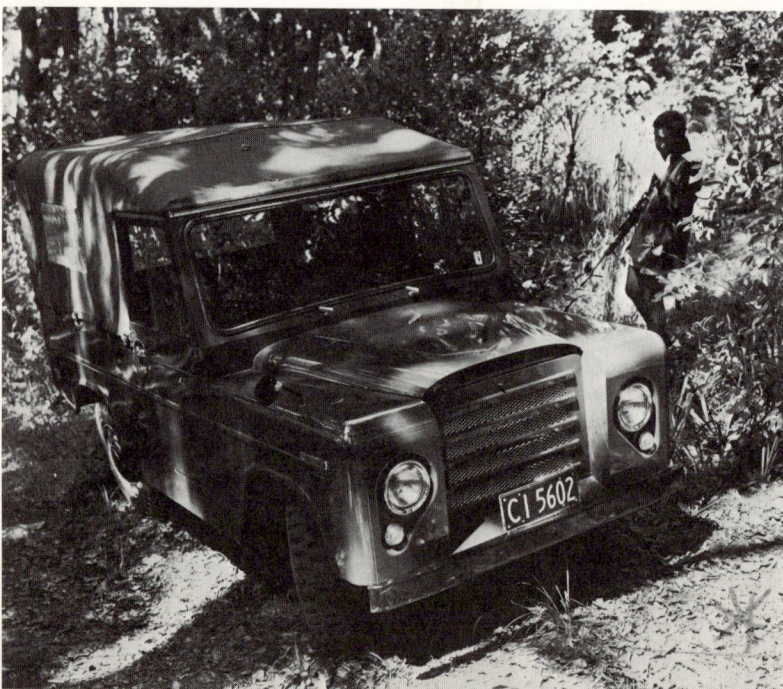

66B Trekka

66A: **Trabant** P601/A 4-seater 4 × 2 military car produced in the 1960s by VEB Sachsenring-Automobilwerke in Zwickau, DDR, mainly for the East German Border Police (hence it was dubbed 'Grenztrabant'). It was based on the contemporary Trabant civilian passenger car, which had a 2-cyl. 2-stroke air-cooled engine and front-wheel drive. The P601/A weighed 645 kg and had a cruising speed of 85 km/h (max. speed 100 km/h). GVW was 1020 kg.

66B: **Trekka** 4 × 2 utility vehicle was introduced by Motor Lines (Bodies) Ltd in New Zealand in 1966. It was based on the chassis of the Skoda Octavia Combi, with 1221-cc 47-bhp (gross) OHV Four engine and 4F1R gearbox. There were eight body styles and a limited-slip diff. was available. Some 3000 units were made until production ceased in early 1973.

66C: **Triumph** Pony was designed in 1965 by the Triumph Motor Co. in Coventry, England, using the engine/transmission unit of their then new 1300 front-wheel drive car. However, the subsequent merger with Rover within the framework of the British Leyland Motor Corp. and therefore the clashing with the well-established Land-Rover precluded its series production. The same applied to Austin's Ant (q.v.) but Triumph sold the Pony's production licence to the Israeli firm of Autocars (q.v.) who manufactured it for several years.

66D: **UAZ**-469B was first announced in 1961 by the Soviet Ulyanovsk Automobile Works. It was intended as a replacement for the GAZ-69AM (q.v.) but it took about 10 years before series production commenced. It seats 7 persons, or 2 plus a load of 600 kg, and weighs 1540 kg. Wheelbase is 2·38 m. The power unit is a 72-bhp 2450-cc OHV Four, driving through a 4F1R × 2 transmission.

67A–D : Research and development of the M151 Series of $\frac{1}{4}$-ton 4 × 4 Utility Trucks, the replacement for the US armed forces' M38 and M38A1 (see Jeep), was initiated in 1950 by the Ordnance Tank-Automotive Command and in 1951 a contract was awarded to the Ford Motor Co. for a concept study. After testing and evaluation of the Ford prototypes (q.v.) a production contract was awarded to Ford in June, 1959 ; production commenced early in the following year. Since then the M151 has been in large-scale production by Ford, Willys and the latter's successors : Kaiser-Jeep, Jeep Corp. and AM General Corp. The M151 has an OHV 4-cyl. engine, 4F1R × 1 transmission and independent coil-spring suspension. The swing axle rear suspension was strengthened in 1964 (M151A1) and changed to the trailing arm configuration in 1970 (M151A2) after many road accidents had happened. These were due to vehicles rolling over on account of the unusual suspension geometry and therefore the vehicle's dangerous handling characteristics. Several kits were devised to adapt the basic vehicle to various special requirements, e.g. side curtains, heater, hard-top, deep water fording, etc. Model M151A1C is a modification for the mounting of the 106-mm Recoilless Rifle. M718 is a front-line ambulance. Experimental modifications have included 6 × 6 and 8 × 8 derivatives. In 1972 a simplified 4 × 4 version with leaf-sprung live axles and 3F1R × 2 transmission was introduced, designated M151A2-LC.

67A: M151 (Ford)

67B M151 (Ford, Willys)

67C M151A1 (Kaiser Jeep)

67D M151A2 (AM General)

VOLKSWAGEN, VOLVO

68A Volkswagen 181

68A/B: Volkswagen 181 field car was introduced in 1969 for military and civilian use. The German *Bundeswehr* soon ordered a first series of 2000 (known as *Pkw 0,4 t*) and other military customers included the Netherlands Air Force and Belgian Air Force. The civilian version is marketed as VW 181 *Mehrzweckwagen* (multi-purpose car). Originally the car had the same engine as the VW 1500 'Beetle'; from 1971 the 1600 engine of 44 bhp (DIN) was used. The rear axle with hub reduction gears originated from the pre-1970 VW Transporter but later models have trailing arm suspension. The bodywork is reminiscent of the wartime VW 82 *Kübelwagen* though roomier and provided with a large front locker which contains, amongst other things, the spare wheel. Like the old *'Kübel'* the VW 181 has only rear-wheel drive. Its maximum speed is 110–115 km/h. Dimensions: wheelbase 2·40 m, overall length 3·78 m, width 1·64 m, height 1·62 m (top erected). Weight 900 kg approx. (gross 1340 kg). It is also made in Mexico (VW Safari).

68B Volkswagen 181

68C: Volvo Model P2104 TP21 military command/radio car, popularly known as *'Sugga'*, appeared in the mid-1950s and consisted of a 4-door 5-seater steel car body on a light but sturdy 4 × 4 truck chassis. In the Swedish Army it was designated *Radiopersonterrängbil 915*. It superseded the Volvo m/43 Model TPV which had been introduced in 1943. The *'Sugga'* had a 3·6-litre L-head Six engine of 90 bhp with 4F1R × 2 transmission and leaf-sprung live axles.
68D: Volvo P2104 Special of about 1965 was a heavy-duty utility car on the same 4 × 4 chassis as the *'Sugga'* (68C). The Swedish armed forces used similar vehicles based on WWII US Dodge ¾-ton 4 × 4 and post-war US Fargo Power Wagon chassis. All these vehicles were superseded by the Volvo Laplander (*q.v.*).

68C Volvo P2104 TP21

68D Volvo P2104 Special

69A Volvo L2304

69A : **Volvo** introduced an entirely new 4 × 4 forward-control off-road vehicle in 1959. Designated Model L2304, it was powered by Volvo's B16A 1·58-litre 4-cyl. 60-bhp car engine, driving the leaf-sprung live axles through a 4F1R × 2 transmission. Two of the prototypes journeyed from Gothenburg, Sweden (Volvo's hometown) to Cape Town; others were tested in Finland, Norway and other countries. Wheelbase was 2·10 m, track 1·30, tyre size 7·00 or 9·00-16. Three types were made: soft-top (shown), steel truck cab and hard-top.

69B : **Volvo** L3314 was the production model, better known as the Laplander. This vehicle had the Volvo B 18A 68-bhp engine but was fundamentally similar to the L2304 (for distinguishing features note air intake below windscreen and revised bumper). There were three basic standard models : L3314SU (shown), L3314PU (truck cab) and L3314HT (hard-top). Experimental models included military 6 × 6 and 8 × 8 derivatives. L3314 production commenced in 1963/64, for civilian and military customers. In Sweden it is popularly known as 'Valpen' (puppy).

69C : **Volvo** L3304 was an interesting normal-control variant of the L3314 Laplander. It first appeared in 1964 and is used by Swedish Army armoured brigades as a mobile mount for their 9-cm anti-tank gun.

69D : **Volvo** 4140 Series, intended to replace the Laplander L3314 models, first appeared in 1969 and comprised 1-ton 4 × 4 (4141) and 1½-ton 6 × 6 (4143) versions. 94-bhp B20B 4-cyl. and 120-bhp B30 6-cyl. engines were used, with 4F1R × 2 transmission and live axles with leaf springs and auxiliary rubber units. An experimental 8 × 8 was also made. Shown is a Model 4141 with hard-top. In 1974 it was announced that production of the earlier Laplander L3314 (69B) would, from 1975, take place in Hungary.

69B Volvo L3314SU Laplander

69C Volvo L3304

69D Volvo 4141

WILLYS, YETI, ZASTAVA, ZAZ

70A Willys Rural

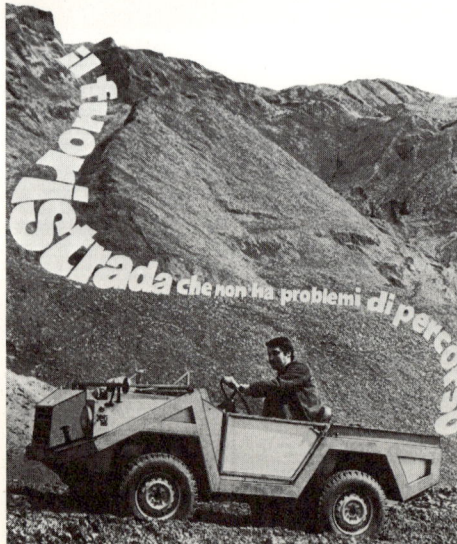

70C Zastava AR51

70B : Yeti 850, an Italian 4 × 4 'mountain buggy', made in 1968 by Delta of Turin, had a 42-bhp Fiat 850 engine, 4F1R × 2 transmission and four-wheel steering. Kerb weight was 825 kg, GVW 1195 kg. It reappeared in 1971 as SAMAS Yeti 903, with the then new 47-bhp Fiat 127 power unit.

70A : Willys Rural Station Wagon was one of several models made by Willys-Overland do Brasil SA of São Paulo, a company which had started assembly (later manufacture) of the Willys Jeep in 1954. The Jeep Station Wagon shown, known as the Rural, first appeared in 1958. Other body styles were also made. In 1967/68 the company merged with Ford Motor do Brasil SA to form Ford-Willys do Brasil SA. The Rural then became a Ford-Willys.

NOTE: Willys-Overland in the USA was bought by the Henry Kaiser industrial empire in 1953 and 10 years later the company was renamed Kaiser Jeep Corporation. In 1970 it became a subsidiary of American Motors, named Jeep Corporation. **Jeep having been a registered trade name for many years the various Willys (and later) Jeep vehicles are in this book dealt with under the marque name Jeep (pages 38–44).**

70C : Zastava AR51 was the Italian Fiat Campagnola (*q.v.*) as licence-produced by the Crvena Zastava (Red Flag) works in Yugoslavia. In addition to the basic model shown there was a 2-stretcher ambulance version (Zastava AR51S). The AR51 could carry 6 persons plus 50 kg or 2 plus 330 kg. Speed range was 7 to 116 km/h.

70D : ZAZ, a light car factory in the Russian Ukraine, produced several small 4 × 2 and 4 × 4 utility vehicles during the 1960s. Model shown (1970) had an air-cooled V-4-cyl. engine, providing a maximum road speed of about 75 km/h. The high ground clearance (0·30 m) and short wheelbase (1·32 m) are noteworthy.

70B Yeti 850

70D ZAZ 969

In addition to the many types of cross-country cars and utility vehicles shown in this book there are some other categories in which there is too much variety for comprehensive coverage. A few typical and representative examples are shown here. Furthermore, several firms in America, Britain, etc. offer kits for off-road/fun cars which the buyer can assemble, using mechanical components of certain popular cars.

71B Dune Buggy (VW/BAC)

71C Three-Wheeled Bike (Maverick)

71A: *All-Terrain Vehicles*, often referred to as ATVs, reputedly originated in Canada in the early 1960s and are among the most ingenious of go-anywhere vehicles. Most ATVs consist of a watertight hull with four, six or eight driven wheels with soft wide low-pressure tyres which obviate springs. A typical example is this 6-wheeled Gatomontes, produced in Barcelona, Spain. It is propelled by a Citroën 3 CV 602-cc engine/gearbox unit with centrifugal clutch. The buoyance of hull and tyres gives an excellent amphibious capability, the spinning tyres providing paddle-wheel-type propulsion. Many vehicles of this type have been made, especially in North America.

71B: *Dune Buggies* are another popular breed. They originated in places such as Arizona and California, and consisted of modified car chassis with large tyres and other modifications. From the early 1950s shortened VW 'Beetle' chassis with bathtub-like 2-seater bodywork have become the most numerous in this category and there are many variations.

71C: *Three-Wheeled Bikes* have appeared in considerable numbers in the USA as snow fun cars. Again, there were and are many variants. Shown is a California-made K & P Mfg. Maverick of the mid-1960s. They are also used in sandy and marshy areas.

71D: *Terräng Axel* 'Oldsmolvo': starting with a wrecked 1953 Oldsmobile 88 car with V8 engine and Hydra-Matic, a Swedish enthusiast built this impressive and unique 4 × 4 off-road machine. It is just one example of numerous 'Specials' built by enterprising individuals all over the world.

71A ATV (Gatomontes)

71D Terräng Axle Special (Olds/Volvo)

ABBREVIATIONS

CID	cubic inches displacement
CR	compression ratio
diff	differential

L-head	side valves
OHV	overhead valves
PTO	power-take off

F-head	inlet-over-exhaust valves
GVW	gross vehicle weight

q.v.	quod vide (which see)
wb	wheelbase